MEASURING CUSTOMER SATISFACTION

Richard F. Gerson, Ph.D.

A FIFTY-MINUTE™ SERIES BOOK

CRISP PUBLICATIONS, INC.
Menlo Park, California

MEASURING CUSTOMER SATISFACTION

Richard F. Gerson, Ph.D.

CREDITS:
Editor: **Brenda Machosky**
Typesetting: **ExecuStaff**
Cover Design: **Carol Harris**
Artwork: **Ralph Mapson**

Copyright © 1993 Crisp Publications, Inc.
Printed in the United States of America by Bawden Printing Company.

English language Crisp books are distributed worldwide. Our major international distributors include:

CANADA: Reid Publishing, Ltd., Box 69559—109 Thomas St., Oakville, Ontario Canada L6J 7R4. TEL: (416) 842-4428; FAX: (416) 842-9327

AUSTRALIA: Career Builders, P.O. Box 1051, Springwood, Brisbane, Queensland, Australia 4127. TEL: 841-1061, FAX: 841-1580

NEW ZEALAND: Career Builders, P.O. Box 571, Manurewa, Auckland, New Zealand. TEL: 266-5276, FAX: 266-4152

JAPAN: Phoenix Associates Co., Mizuho Bldg. 2-12-2, Kami Osaki, Shinagawa-Ku, Tokyo 141, Japan. TEL: 3-443-7231, FAX: 3-443-7640

Selected Crisp titles are also available in other languages. Contact International Rights Manager Tim Polk at (800) 442-7477 for more information.

Library of Congress Catalog Card Number 92-054368
Gerson, Richard F.
Measuring Customer Satisfaction
ISBN 1-56052-178-3

This book is printed on recyclable paper with soy ink.

PREFACE

Everyone is aware of the importance of satisfying customers. You can't get away from the fact that reporters, authors, consultants, and everyone else is telling you that you must satisfy your customers in order to be competitive.

Yet, while these same people tell you what to do and some tell you how to do it, few if any tell you how to determine how well you are doing it. You only know how well you are satisfying your customers if you measure their satisfaction levels.

This book is designed to help you do just that. It was written for everyone, from the business owner to the first line supervisor to the customer contact person. The book describes why it is important to measure customer satisfaction, its link to quality and quality improvement measurement tools, and how your company can benefit from knowing about customer satisfaction.

Most approaches at satisfaction measurement are haphazard, at best. Measurement, along with customer service management and services marketing, must be an integrated part of an overall system. The measurement component shows you and tells you how well you are managing your customer service functions, and it also guides you in your marketing efforts. Crucial to your success in measuring quality and customer satisfaction is knowing what to measure, when to measure it, how to measure it, how to analyze the data, and then what to do with your results. This book is your guide.

The first part of the book focuses on defining customer satisfaction, the costs of poor service and poor quality and how these affect your company, and how to develop a superior customer service system. The second part of the book covers why you must measure quality as part of your customer satisfaction program and then teaches you how to use the 7 basic quality improvement measurement tools. Part 3 covers research methods in customer satisfaction, including data collection techniques, measurement techniques and analysis. Part 4 discusses in greater detail the importance of managing customer satisfaction, and the appendixes give you samples of customer satisfaction surveys and reports.

Measuring customer satisfaction, and the associated quality of your product or service, is necessary to your success, but not sufficient for it. You must then know how to market the fact that your customers are satisfied with what you do for them. This point is touched upon only briefly in this book, and you can find much more detail on it in my other Crisp Publications book, *Beyond Customer Service.*

One final point before you get into the book. You will soon find that quality improvement and even customer satisfaction may not be enough to keep you competitive and make you profitable. You will eventually need something more. You will need to WOW and DELIGHT your customers all the time so that they become your best supporters. You will have to adapt and modify your customer service programs and systems to achieve this, but one thing is certain.

You will always have to measure quality and customer satisfaction to determine where you are, are you doing enough, is what you are doing satisfactory in the eyes and minds of the customers, and where you should be going next. This book will help you.

ABOUT THIS BOOK

Measuring Customer Satisfaction is not like most books. It has a unique "self-paced" format that encourages a reader to become personally involved. Designed to be "read with a pencil," there are an abundance of exercises, activities, assessments and cases that invite participation.

The objective of this book is to help business owners and managers identify customer service needs, use quantifiable methods (as described in the exercises) to assess whether the needs have been met and resolve potential problem areas in an accurate and objective manner.

Measuring Customer Satisfaction (and the other self-improvement books listed in the back of this book) can be used effectively in a number of ways. Here are some possibilities:

Individual Study.   Because the book is self-instructional, all that is needed is a quiet place, some time and a pencil. Completing the activities and exercises should provide not only valuable feedback, but also practical ideas about measuring and improving customer satisfaction.

Workshops and Seminars.   The book is ideal for preassigned reading prior to a workshop or seminar. With the basics in hand, the quality of participation should improve. More time can be spent on concept extensions and applications during the program. The book is also effective when distributed at the beginning of a session.

Remote Location Training.   Copies can be sent to those not able to attend "home office" training sessions.

Informal Study Groups.   Thanks to the format, brevity and low cost, this book is ideal for "brown-bag" or other informal group sessions.

There are other possibilities that depend on the objectives of the user. One thing for sure, even after it has been read, this book will serve as excellent reference material which can be easily reviewed. Good luck!

ABOUT THE AUTHOR

Richard F. Gerson, Ph.D., CMC, is president of Gerson Goodson, Inc., a marketing, management and training consulting firm. Dr. Gerson is a nationally renowned speaker and corporate trainer who has presented to tens of thousands of people at numerous regional, national and international conventions in the areas of sales, marketing, customer service, quality improvement and communications skills.

Dr. Gerson received his Ph.D. from Florida State University in 1978 and established his company in early 1979. His clients include individual entrepreneurs as well as Fortune 500 companies. He has consulted with and trained many professional organizations to enhance their marketing efforts and the service, productivity and performance of their members.

Dr. Gerson has written books, including *Writing and Implementing a Marketing Plan* and *Beyond Customer Service, Measuring Customer Satisfaction* and the *Marketing Strategies for Small Business,* all published by Crisp Publications. He also has written over 200 articles in professional journals, popular and trade magazines, newspapers and newsletters, and is a much sought-after speaker at numerous national and international conventions.

Dr. Gerson can be reached by writing:

Richard F. Gerson, Ph.D.
Gerson Goodson, Inc.
PO Box 1534
Safety Harbor, FL 34695

DEDICATION:

This book is dedicated to my wife, Robbie, and our children, Michael and Mitchell, who constantly remind me to pay attention to the little things in life because it's the little things that make a quality life worth living.

CONTENTS

INTRODUCTION

Measuring Customer Satisfaction was written in response to numerous requests from clients and seminar attendees who knew it was important to measure quality and satisfaction, but did not know how to measure it or did not know what to do with whatever measurements they collected. The book is written to clear up and resolve these potential problem areas and to give everyone, business owners, managers, consultants and employees, an understanding of the importance of the measurement process along with some methods and techniques to quantify their performance.

Not everything we do in business can be measured. However, when it comes to providing quality products and services and satisfying customers, we must know exactly how we are doing. Measurement, and appropriate follow-up, is essential to success in today's business climate. Research shows that by simply measuring performance, productivity improves, quality can improve and levels of customer satisfaction can improve. Now, with the measurement techniques described in this book, you can accurately and objectively determine how well you are doing and what else you must do to meet and exceed your customer's expectations of your product or service.

You can use this book in a number of ways.

► **Individualized Instruction:** The book is designed for you to teach yourself. Take your time as you go through it. Follow the exercises carefully and do each one. Practice them over and over again. The more familiarity you develop with the measurement techniques and how to use them, the more successful you will be in improving your quality and customer service.

► **Workshops and Seminars:** The book can be used, and has been, as the basis for workshops and seminars on measurement techniques. The workshop facilitator can follow the book exactly, or modify the approach using the various sections in the book. Participants will find the book very useful during the workshop, and also as a study guide and reference manual after the workshop has been completed.

► **Remote Training:** The book can be sent to remote locations for training purposes and users of the book can then be tested for knowledge of its contents. The book can also be used as a workbook for a teleconference or video conference.

INTRODUCTION (continued)

The book was written for you. Your success in measuring quality and customer satisfaction will be determined by how often you use the methods and techniques described in the book. You may not ever perfect all the techniques, but constant use and practice will help you to continuously improve in them. You will benefit, your business will benefit and your customers will benefit.

Richard F. Gerson, Ph.D.

P A R T

I

Customer Satisfaction

WELL YES, MADAME... BUT WE **DID** REMOVE THE STAIN.

WHAT IS CUSTOMER SATISFACTION?

There is a great deal of information being published today and discussed on the topic of total quality management, continuous quality improvement, customer service and customer satisfaction. Proponents of these topics or approaches to conducting business tend to emphasize the importance of conforming to specifications, keeping processes in control, meeting requirements, giving customers what they want and handling complaints effectively. Despite the proliferation of books, articles, videos, seminars and conferences on these subjects and approaches, none of them is central to a successful business.

The thing that counts today is **customer satisfaction.** If your customer is not satisfied, he or she will stop doing business with you. All the things you do to achieve quality and provide excellent service are not important at all if you do not work to satisfy the customer.

Just what is customer satisfaction? It is the customer's perception that his or her expectations have been met or surpassed. You buy something and you expect it to work properly. If it does, you are satisfied. If it does not, you are dissatisfied. Now, it is up to the seller to find a way to fix the problem so that you can become satisfied. When the fix occurs to your approval, you are satisfied. When it does not, you will "vote with your feet" and take your business elsewhere.

Satisfied Customers Buy More, and More Often

It is a simple truth. Satisfied customers do more business with you more often. They purchase more each time around, and they purchase more often. They also refer their family and friends to you. The link between sales, service, satisfaction and profits is direct. The more a customer is satisfied, the more he or she spends. The more customers spend, the more you sell. And usually, when you sell more, your profits are greater.

WHICH IS MORE IMPORTANT: QUALITY, SERVICE, SATISFACTION OR RETENTION?

This question must be answered by your business to ensure your success. We will discuss measuring all these aspects in a moment. For now, you must realize that they are all important, each in a distinct way.

Quality and service are the means to the ends of satisfaction and retention. Your overall goal in business should not be to produce a quality product or service, or to provide superior customer service. Your main goal should be to produce a satisfied and loyal customer who will stay with you over time. Therefore, providing high quality and superior customer service are givens when you consider your ultimate goal.

In my previous book, *Beyond Customer Service,* I focused on the importance of providing superior customer service and then using that as a marketing technique to foster customer loyalties and retention. The goal of that book was to offer you many methods to keep customers coming back for life. This book will teach you how to measure your quality and service activities in order to determine your levels of customer satisfaction and to help you develop programs that increase customer retention.

What Gets Measured Gets Done

This is a very true axiom. Whenever you measure something, it gets performed, completed, and usually, improved upon. That is why measurement techniques are so important to quality improvement. It is also why so many companies have begun measuring the satisfaction levels of their customers.

When you have a quantifiable number, or measure, to put on a behavior, people can see exactly what effect that behavior is having on their own and the company's performance. Asking customers to rate you on your levels of quality and service, and their level of satisfaction, virtually guarantees that you will work to improve your efforts in these areas.

Later sections in this book will discuss how to develop measurement techniques and programs for quality and customer satisfaction. For now, it is sufficient to say that measurement is the critical component in determining if your service programs and overall performance are meeting or exceeding customer needs.

Defining Customer Satisfaction

The definition of customer satisfaction is very simple. A customer is satisfied whenever his or her needs, real or perceived, are met or exceeded. So, how do you know what the customer needs, wants and expects? You ask! That's right. It's very simple. You just ask, and then you provide what the customer wants and more.

> *Customer Satisfaction: When a product or service meets or exceeds a customer's expectations, the customer is usually satisfied.*

Defining Quality

Quality is a little harder to define than customer satisfaction simply because of the many definitions that all the experts have promoted and publicized. For our purposes, quality is based on the perception of the customer. Therefore, quality is defined as whatever the customer perceives as quality.

> *Quality: Whatever the customer says it is.*

These definitions may seem very simplistic to you, especially the one for quality. They are simple, and elegant, by design. Using these definitions will now enable you to accurately measure the quality and customer satisfaction levels in your company or organization. Your measurement objectives are simply to find out what your customer thinks quality is and how he or she defines satisfaction. Then, you build your measurement techniques around those objectives and definitions.

WHICH IS MORE IMPORTANT: QUALITY, SERVICE, SATISFACTION OR RETENTION? (continued)

In the spaces below, write out the definitions of quality (or quality improvement) and customer satisfaction as they currently exist for your company. Then, below that, write these definitions in terms defined or described by your customers. Now, compare the difference, if any, and determine which set of definitions will work better for you in the long run.

CURRENT DEFINITIONS:

    Quality (Quality Improvement):

_____

_____

_____

    Customer Satisfaction:

_____

_____

_____

CUSTOMER DEFINITIONS:

    Quality (Quality Improvement):

_____

_____

_____

    Customer Satisfaction:

_____

_____

_____

THE COSTS OF POOR SERVICE AND POOR QUALITY

In *Beyond Customer Service,* I gave you a formula for calculating the cost of poor service. This formula included: Lost Customer Revenue, which is the money you will lose when customers begin doing business with your competitors because you gave them poor service; Lost Opportunity Revenue, which is the potential money you will lose when customers are dissatisfied, or when former customers tell their friends not to do business with you; and Customer Replacement Costs, which is the cost of acquiring new customers to replace the ones you lost. To calculate the cost of poor service, you need to know your annual revenues, your current number of customers and your current acquisition costs. You then plug the information into sections of the formula to determine how much money you are losing due to poor service.

Another way to calculate the cost of poor service is to determine how many customers you lose on an annual basis, and what their average revenue value is to your company. Then, you multiply that by your expected or realized profit margin for the year, and add in any other costs such as account closing costs, expenses related to attempted recovery such as salaries and overhead, and again, lost opportunity revenue. Here is an example of the cost of losing customers.

Number of Lost Accounts	1000
Average Revenue per Account	× $1000.00
Total Lost Annual Revenues	**$1,000,000.00**
Lost Profits (assume 10% profit margin)	× .10
Total Lost Profits	**$100,000.00**
Closing and Recovery Costs per Account	$50.00
Number of Lost Accounts (again)	× 1000
Total Closing and Recovery Costs	**$50,000.00**
TOTAL COSTS OF LOST ACCOUNTS	**$150,000.00**
TOTAL COSTS OF POOR SERVICE	**$1,150,000.00**

THE COST OF POOR QUALITY

Calculating the cost of poor quality is slightly more difficult than determining the cost of poor service, although arguments can be made that the same formula could be used. After all, if you provide a poor quality product or service, you will lose current customers and potential future customers.

Here are some other things to consider when you determine the cost of quality in your organization. First, there are four factors that you can put a price on to identify your cost of poor quality:

- **Performance Cost**—The cost of doing it right the first time. This is the cost associated with producing something that is error free and that will not have to be redone or reworked.

- **Rework or Failure Cost**—The cost of doing something over again. Repair, rework and correcting failures can account for up to 50% of your cost of doing business. Another item that must be included in this factor is the cost of making restitution or amends to the customer.

- **Detection Costs**—The cost of detecting or finding quality problems. These include inspection costs, salaries, and any other extra procedures that contribute to detecting problems before they go out the door.

- **Prevention Costs**—The cost of identifying quality impairments before they reach what is normally called the quality inspection or quality control stage. Prevention costs are minimized when every worker is capable of inspecting his or her own work. These costs can also be hidden in the detection cost factor.

These are the four factors you must investigate to determine your cost of poor quality. Now, quality itself never costs, it pays. You have to determine how much it will pay you to provide quality products and services by checking your position in these five key areas:

- **Price**—Higher quality and better service allows you to charge more for your goods and services. Research supports this position.

- **Profitability**—True quality, which is preventing errors by doing it right the first time, according to expectations established by customers, leads to cost savings and increased sales. The result, especially when combined with higher prices, is increased profitability.

- **Market Share**—Research again supports the position that higher quality means greater market share. Even if you are charging more for your products or services, people are willing to pay the price simply because they know they are getting quality and value for their money.

- **Cost**—Improved quality decreases production costs because you are only doing something once. Poor quality increases production costs because you always have to do it over again or make reparations to your customers in hopes of keeping them.

- **Marketing and Advertising**—The relative costs here will decrease for two reasons. The first is that you will be selling more, so your effective cost per sale will decrease even if you increase your advertising expenditures. The second is that your word-of-mouth marketing and referral business will increase, thereby lowering your external advertising costs.

Another thing you must consider about the cost of poor quality is your customer's cost for doing business with you. How much time, effort and money must a customer expend to make the first purchase from you, and then come back and get the product repaired or replaced? These costs must also be figured into your calculations.

When you combine all the factors related to the cost of poor customer service and the cost of poor quality, you begin to realize how important it is to provide the best of both. The dollars you can lose are enormous, and they cannot be made up through cost-cutting measures and expense cost containment. It is a rare company that can improve customer service and quality by cutting costs. However, most companies that improve customer service and quality also realize a cost savings and an increase in profitability.

THE RELATIONSHIP AMONG QUALITY, SERVICE AND SATISFACTION

It should be quite obvious by now that there is a distinct relationship among quality, customer service and customer satisfaction. This becomes even more apparent when you consider that quality and service are whatever the customer says they are, *not* what you say they are. And satisfaction is the customer's perception that his or her expectations have been met.

Therefore, if you provide the first two according to your customer's definitions, the third will follow. Plus, satisfied customers will bring you more customers, who will then bring you more customers, and the referral cycle will continue.

Fill in the following chart to help you graphically depict these relationships as they affect your business today, and in the years to come.

For the quality rating, give yourself a number based on what you perceive your level of quality to be, with 10 being the best. The customer satisfaction level should be determined by your surveys and interviews. If you are not doing these with your customers, don't worry: This book will help you to develop these programs. The number of lost customers and acquisition costs can be obtained from your financial records. The price of your product or service as well as your profit margin can also be obtained from your records. Advertising costs include everything you spend on communicating with the public. Your market rank is your position within your industry and your market share is the percentage of that position.

Complete this chart and refer to it often. You will begin to see how much you improve as you improve your quality and customer service.

Category	Today	Next Year	3 Years	5 Years
Quality Rating (1–10)				
Customer Satisfaction Level				
# of Lost Customers				
Acquisition Costs				
Price				
Profitability				
Marketing/ Advertising Costs				
Market Rank				
Market Share				

DEVELOPING A CUSTOMER SERVICE SYSTEM

Before you can measure how well you are providing customer service, you need to have a customer service system in place. Otherwise, you will not have a way to measure customer satisfaction. Here is a seven-step approach to developing a successful customer service system followed by some techniques you can use to implement customer service and quality improvement within your company.

Step 1: Total Management Commitment

Customer service and quality improvement programs will only succeed when there is total management commitment, and this commitment must begin at the top. The president, CEO, chairman of the board or owner must develop and communicate a clear vision of what the service quality system is going to be, how it is going to be implemented, what the staff should expect when implementing it, how it will be used to satisfy and retain customers and how it will be supported over time. This process of total management commitment must begin with a vision statement or mission statement related to service quality. Write yours in the space below.

_____

_____

_____

_____

_____

_____

_____

_____

Step 2: Know Your Customers (Intimately)

You must do everything possible to get to know your customers intimately and to understand them totally. Some people suggest that you get to know your customers better than they know themselves. This means knowing their likes and dislikes in regards to your business; the changes they may want you to make; their needs, wants and expectations (now and in the future); what motivates them to buy or change suppliers; what you must do to satisfy them, retain them and make them loyal. You learn all this by simply asking your customers.

When you have learned about your customers and you think you know them as well as you know yourself, you must learn about them all over again. Their needs change daily, even hourly, and you must know how to satisfy those needs. Their requirements and expectations change also, and you must be able to meet and exceed those expectations. Knowing your customers intimately, and on an ongoing basis, requires that you keep in constant contact with them. Call them regularly. Write to them. Invite them to lunch or to your office or facility. Find out exactly what they are doing, what they need, and what they want you to do for them. This constant contact will help you develop the retention and loyalty you need because they know you are interested in them.

Step 3: Develop Standards of Service Quality Performance

Customer service, quality and service quality appear to be intangible items because they are based on perception. However, they do have tangible and visible aspects that you can manage and measure. For example, customers dislike waiting for a telephone to be answered or being placed on hold for a long period of time. How many rings does it take for your phone to be answered, and how long do you place your customers on hold without getting back to them to tell them what is going on? How many transfers or how many steps through an automatic call-distribution menu does it take for a customer to get a question answered or a complaint resolved? How long does it take to process and ship an order, and is it shipped correctly the first time? What is your policy on customer returns, refunds, exchanges and complaints?

These are all tangible aspects of service quality and they can be measured. If you have any doubts about what to measure, just ask your customers. They will tell you (perhaps not directly or exactly) what they are looking for and how they judge service quality. And since service quality and satisfaction only exist in the minds of the customers, you should develop your standards and measurement systems to meet their perceptions.

DEVELOPING A CUSTOMER SERVICE SYSTEM (continued)

Step 4: Hire, Train and Compensate Good Staff

Superior customer service and quality performance that result in customer satisfaction and retention can only be provided by competent, qualified people. Your service quality is only as good as the people who deliver it. If you want your business to be good to people, and that is a requirement for success in today's business environment, then you must hire good people.

Once hired, train them extensively to provide superior customer service and do things right the first time. Be sure they understand your company's standards of service quality performance and the customer's expectations of service quality. Train them in their own jobs and train them in other jobs as well. Let them experience being a customer of your company; then have them make suggestions for improving the treatment of customers.

Once they are trained, compensate them well. You are now aware of the costs associated with losing a customer and acquiring new ones. The same formula holds true for recruiting, hiring and training new staff. The acquisition costs can be staggering. Train them well and compensate them well. After all, they are your company's initial contact with the buying public. Your employees are your company in the eyes and ears of your customers. If they give bad service, the customer perceives the entire company as giving bad service.

Finally, empower your people to make decisions and do the right thing to satisfy your customers. The staff should not have to look for you or a manager every time a customer asks a question, has a return or a complaint or just needs a problem solved. There are legions of stories about empowered employees who made decisions that were against company policy but that satisfied and retained a customer, with the end result of both the business and the customer winning. If you are going to place people in customer-contact positions, give them the authority that goes with this tremendous responsibility. They must be able to do whatever it takes to satisfy the customer.

Step 5: Reward Service Quality Accomplishments

Always recognize, reward and reinforce superior service quality performances. Do this for your employees and your customers. Provide psychological, and sometimes financial, incentives for your people. Help them motivate themselves to do even better. Broadcast and make a big deal about all types of service accomplishments that result in more satisfied customers. Recognize and reward even the small wins in a manner similar to what you would use for the major accomplishments.

Also, reward your customers for good customer behavior. Everyone wants to be appreciated and made to feel important, especially your customers. Provide them with recognition and appreciation just as you would your employees. This will motivate them to refer more business to you and to be more loyal to you.

Step 6: Stay Close To Your Customers

Even though you have gotten to know your customers intimately in Step 2, you must now do everything possible to stay close to them. Keep in touch with them in any and every way possible. Invite them for site visits. Go visit them. Send them letters, cards, newsletters, published articles that would be of interest to them. Conduct continuous research to learn about their changing needs and expectations.

Ask them questions right after they make a purchase. Ask them why they did not make a purchase. Mail them questionnaires and other types of surveys. Call them up on the telephone and ask them how you can do a better job for them. Get them involved in your business on customer councils, advisory boards, focus groups, and job swapping. Do whatever it takes to stay close to your customers and continue to build and maintain this valuable relationship.

Your relationship with the customer really solidifies after the purchase is made. Let them know you care about them and that you will support their purchase. Make sure they are satisfied, and find out what you must do to maintain that satisfaction and loyalty. Do everything in your power to keep your name in their mind and to keep their perception of your service quality at the highest level possible.

DEVELOPING A CUSTOMER SERVICE SYSTEM (continued)

Step 7: Work Toward Continous Improvement

Now that you have friendly and accessible customer service systems, have hired and trained the best people for the job and have learned everything you can about your customers, you cannot rest. No system or program is perfect, least of all one that is based on a person's perceptions as is the case for service quality. Therefore, you must continually work to improve your customer service and performance quality.

Customers who are initially satisfied with their purchases will perceive your attempts at continuous service quality improvement as something very positive. They may even want to help. Welcome them with open arms. They are your best source of information about how to get better in their eyes and minds. Plus, when you implement their recommendations and suggestions, they perceive that you value them even more. The result is that they will do more business with you, which leads to more satisfied customers, a happier staff and greater profits.

The Customer's Perspective

These seven steps will help you develop a customer service system for your business. The key is to develop this system from the customer's perspective. It should be easy for the customer to access and use, and everything that is done within the system should be done to satisfy the customer. The system is not to be set up to make it easier for your staff to provide service. If your staff has to work a little harder to make it easier for the customer, then so be it. The results will be more satisfied customers and more business.

Service quality pays, it does not cost. If you work to provide the best possible service quality, as defined by your customers, you will have the most loyal and satisfied customers in your industry. When this occurs, the growth, expansion and increased profitability of your business will take care of themselves.

FIVE TECHNIQUES TO IMPLEMENT SUPERIOR SERVICE QUALITY

Here are five ways to implement a service quality program in your company. These techniques will work to improve the quality of the products and services you sell to customers and the level of customer service you provide. Remember that the key to satisfied customers is having them perceive that you have met or exceeded their expectations in a specific situation.

1. Add Value

Give them something more than they were expecting. If you do this, you have already exceeded their expectations and put them on the path to becoming a satisfied customer.

2. Train Your Staff in Internal Quality Measurement Techniques

Your staff must be trained to identify when and where quality problems are occurring and the steps they need to take to correct them before the customer sees any mistakes. Statistical-measurement tools and quality standards of performance are the foundation for making this technique work successfully. Also, have your staff check and re-check their own work, rather than hiring quality inspectors. Finally, you personally must inspect what you expect, so work with employees to set their performance standards and then catch them doing something *right*.

3. Constant Contact

Customers who are communicated with on a regular basis feel cared for, and they are more likely to forgive isolated or intermittent errors on your part. Keep in constant contact with your customers through newsletters, thank-you cards, birthday and holiday cards, and telephone calls.

4. Reward Programs

Customers are just as happy to receive rewards as are your employees. Recognize and reward the efforts of customers when they make additional purchases from you, when they make exceedingly large purchases from you, and when they refer new customers to you.

FIVE TECHNIQUES TO IMPLEMENT SUPERIOR SERVICE QUALITY (continued)

5. Strategic Alliances and Partnerships

All of these techniques should be proactive, and this is probably the most proactive of all. Make your customers your partners, either in a literal or figurative sense. When people have a psychological or financial stake in a venture, they put more effort into making it work. Have your customers visit your office or facility, do a rigorous inspection, and make suggestions on how you can improve your service quality. Invite your customers to be on your advisory board or your board of directors. Their insight will help you be a better provider of goods and services.

Now that you have the ability to develop a successful customer service system and make it work, you are ready to measure your service quality efforts and your level of customer satisfaction. However, before you learn ''how'' to actually do the research and the measurements, you must understand ''why'' you are doing them.

P A R T

II

Measuring Quality and Customer Satisfaction

WHY WE MEASURE QUALITY AND CUSTOMER SATISFACTION

Before you can measure something, you must know what you are measuring and why. The following material will introduce you to the reasons for measuring quality and customer satisfaction. When you know why you are doing this, and then you do it, implementing the results of your measurement program will proceed more smoothly.

Your measurement program must answer the who, what, when, where, how and why questions that are essential for success.

- **Who** will measure quality? The answer is everyone.

- **What** must be measured? Everything and anything that affects the customer.

- **When** must you measure? All the time.

- **Where** do you measure? Throughout the entire company and every process that has an effect on customer satisfaction and quality.

- **How** do you measure? You establish performance standards and criteria that are quantifiable and that you can evaluate your performance against by using hard numbers and data.

- **Why** do you measure? To learn how to improve quality and increase customer satisfaction.

The following pages outline the seven basic reasons for conducting these measurements.

Reason #1: To Learn About Customer Perceptions

Customers are individuals, and each person will perceive things differently in the same situation. While many measurement programs attempt to get at mass averages from which they will build or rebuild their quality and customer service programs, it is imperative that you at least consider identifying each customer's individual perceptions.

The perceptions you are trying to identify include: what they look for in a business such as yours; why they do business in your industry; what has caused them to change suppliers or providers in the past; what might make them change again in the future and how soon; what are their criteria for acceptable service quality performance; what must they receive to be minimally satisfied; what must you do to make them extremely satisfied; and what must you do for them so they will continue to do business with you.

Use the chart on page 25 to fill in what you know about your customers with respect to these perceptions. Also, there are several blank spaces so you can add to this list. Feel free to modify the list as you see fit.

Perceptions To Identify	Your Knowledge
What Customers Look For	
Why Customers Do Business in the Industry	
Reasons for Most Recent Change of Suppliers	
Possible Reasons for Future Change	
Criteria for Acceptable Service Quality	
Criteria for Minimally Satisfied	
Criteria for Exceptionally Satisfied	
Criteria for Retention and Repurchase	

Reason #2: To Determine Customer Needs, Wants, Requirements and Expectations

Your customer satisfaction measurements not only must determine how customers feel about the product or service they purchased and the service they received, the measurement must also identify what the customers need and want from you. You must also find out what they require of you in the way of product/manufacturing specifications or program content, as well as what they expect you to provide during the overall sale and service encounter.

It is vitally important to the success of your measurement program that you learn about customers' current and future needs. Too many companies ask customers about a recent purchase without ever trying to find out why they purchased it, what personal and psychological need the purchase satisfied, how they plan to use the purchase, what they expect from the purchase and what they expect their needs to be in the future.

For example, let's say you build mousetraps, and you have just built the best mousetrap the world has ever seen. Now someone once said that if you build a better mousetrap, the world (read customers) will beat a path to your door. That is assuming they need, want and require a better mousetrap. If your customers have no need for mousetraps, now or in the future, they will not buy them from you. So now you have the world's greatest mousetrap and no customers.

When you measure customer satisfaction, also measure what they need, want, require and expect from you, and why.

Reason #3: To Close the Gaps

There are many gaps that exist between customers and providers, and measuring these gaps is the only way to close them. All the gaps are based on differences in perception between what the business believed it had provided and what the customer perceived to have received. Here is a list of several of the more important gaps that have been identified through research.

► **The gap between what a business thinks a customer wants and what the customer actually wants**

This is like having a company build that better mousetrap and inform the public it needs to buy it when all the customer wants is a piece of cheese.

You and your business can never know what a customer truly wants unless you directly ask the customer. Use your measurement tools to inform the customers of what you think they may want, and then allow them to tell you specifically what they want. The difference in perceptions is the gap you must close here.

▶ **The gap between what a business thinks a customer has bought and what a customer perceives has been received**

It really doesn't matter what the business sold to the customer if the customer perceives he or she did not receive exactly what was supposed to be purchased. A mule instead of a horse, a regular stereo instead of a surround-sound stereo, or a training program that promises one set of results yet the customer believes those results were not achieved—all create this type of gap.

The gap exists because the customer does not perceive the purchase in the same way as the business perceives the purchase. Even if the business is right, the customer will feel cheated, and dissatisfied. It is up to the business to close that gap and make certain the customer feels satisfied.

▶ **The gap between the service quality the business believes it is providing and what the customer perceives is being provided**

This is very similar to the preceding problem in that the business believes one thing and the customer believes another. This gap usually occurs when the business has certain customer service policies that it tends not to change for each individual customer and neglects to inform the customer of the policies. Thus, both parties are making decisions without benefit of all the available information. The customer does not know the business has certain policies and feels slighted by the apparent lack of service. The business may never know that the customer feels slighted.

▶ **The gap between customers' expectations of service quality and actual performance**

The problems that exist if this gap occurs are quite obvious. If you do not know what your customers expect of you, and you give them something completely different, or even slightly different, you can be sure they will not be satisfied. You must do everything possible to learn what your customers expect of you, and then deliver it to their satisfaction.

▶ **The gap between marketing promises and actual delivery**

There are many times a company promises to deliver a certain level of service quality and is unable to meet that promise. Making the promise has raised the level of expectation of the customer, and then not delivering on it has created an unhappy customer. The simplest way to close this gap is to underpromise and overdeliver.

REASON #3: TO CLOSE THE GAPS (continued)

Closing these gaps is critical to your success in satisfying and retaining customers. Following are 10 questions you can ask to help you close these gaps and hopefully, make sure they never exist.

1. Have you asked your customers what they need, want and expect from you?

2. Is your company committed to providing superior service quality based on your customer research?

3. Do you have a clear idea of how your customers make purchase decisions?

4. Do you know what criteria your customers use to define quality and determine if they are satisfied?

5. Have you overpromised on your delivery capabilities?

6. Do your customers perceive you can meet their needs and expectations?

7. Do you understand your customers' needs and expectations?

8. Do you have a performance-measurement system in place to help identify customer needs, wants, requirements and expectations?

9. Do you have a recovery program in place to turn a dissatisfied customer around or to recapture a lost customer?

10. Do your standards of service quality performance and customer satisfaction match the perceptual standards developed by your customers?

You can probably add several more questions to this list from your own experiences. These 10 will serve as an introductory guide for you as you attempt to close the service quality gaps that may exist.

Reason #4: To Inspect What You Expect In Order to Improve Service Quality and Customer Satisfaction

You must set standards of performance, inform your staff and your customers of those standards and then measure your actual performance against those standards. When you set goals for your business based on your customers' requirements and expectations, and then you publicly measure your performance toward those goals, you will have an excellent chance of improving both your quality and service.

The improvement comes from knowing where you are compared to where you want to be or should be, and then taking the steps, based on the measurements, to improve your performance. Since your standards were developed in conjunction with customer perceptions, your meeting or exceeding those standards, as well as falling short, will give you a good indicator of how satisfied your customers will be and what you must do in the future.

Reason #5: Because Improved Performance Leads to Increased Profits

While there is no guarantee that this will occur, it is a safe assumption that if you improve your service quality performance and delivery, you will probably benefit from increased profits. More people will want to buy from you, thereby increasing the volume contribution to profits. Also, as your level of service quality goes up along with levels of customer satisfaction, you can conceivably charge more money for your goods and services. This increased price, combined with the decreased costs you get from quality processes, will also lead to greater profitability.

Reason #6: To Learn How You Are Doing and Where You Go From Here

There are many very good reasons to measure your service-quality performance and customer-satisfaction levels. This one may be the most important of all. While you must know what gaps may exist and how to close them, what your customers need and expect and how they perceive the world, you need to know how you are doing right here, right now. Plus, you must be able to gather information on what you should be doing in the future.

Customer research will provide you with this information. Customers will tell you if you are satisfying them now and what you must do to satisfy them in the future. They will also tell you if you need to change your business strategy and/or business direction. Measuring customers' perceptions of service quality and satisfaction levels is essential to your business success.

Reason #7: To Apply the Process of Continuous Improvement

Somehow this theme keeps coming up. If you do not try continuously to improve your service offerings, someone else will, and then your customers will be their customers. You must measure everything you do in relation to your own production of goods and services and your delivery of them to your customers. Ask your buying customers as well as your employees how you can be better at what you do. Take their answers, suggestions and recommendations and implement them within your business. Then ask again, and again. And keep making those incremental improvements.

Remember that your goal is to establish long-term relationships with satisfied customers, and you do this by understanding and identifying their needs, meeting and exceeding their expectations, closing or removing any perceptual gaps that may exist between what the business believes was delivered and the customers believe was received, and trying continuously to improve your service quality efforts a little bit at a time.

THE BENEFITS OF MEASURING QUALITY AND CUSTOMER SATISFACTION

The primary benefit of a measurement program is that it provides people with immediate, meaningful and objective feedback. They can see how they are doing right now, compare it to some standard of excellence or performance, and decide what they must do to improve on that measurement. Have you ever asked yourself why basketball is so popular? It is because the player knows immediately if he or she succeeded. Performance is measured by the ball going through the basket or not, and the player is motivated to try again. This occurs whether or not the shot was successful.

Measurement provides people with a sense of accomplishment, a feeling of achievement. Measurements can also form the basis for a reward system that can only be successful if it is based on objective and quantifiable data. How will you know which employees or work teams to reward for improving quality and increasing customer satisfaction if you cannot, or do not, measure their performance.

The benefits of measuring quality and customer satisfaction can be summed up in these five items:

1. Measurement provides people with a sense of achievement and accomplishment, which will then be translated into superior service to customers.

2. Measurement provides people with a baseline standard of performance and a possible standard of excellence which they must try to achieve, which will lead to improved quality and increased customer satisfaction.

3. Measurement offers a performer immediate feedback, especially when the customer is measuring the performer or the providing company.

4. Measurement tells you what you must do to improve quality and customer satisfaction and how you must do it. This information can also come directly from the customer.

5. Measurement motivates people to perform and achieve higher levels of productivity.

A FINAL THOUGHT ON MEASURING QUALITY AND CUSTOMER SATISFACTION

The concepts of continuous incremental improvement, superior customer service, and high quality are all related to customer satisfaction. However, if you have the chance to make a quantum leap in any of these areas to increase customer satisfaction, do it. Don't ever get locked into the mindset that you must do things a little bit at a time. If the situation presents itself for a major breakthrough in service quality or customer satisfaction, go for it. Also, teach your employees, associates and partners to go for it. You don't want to get locked into another "process" that is governed by policies and procedures that say you must make small, incremental improvements in order to be effective and successful. When the big jump presents itself, JUMP.

Remember this. The reason WHY you measure is to learn what you must do to improve. HOW you measure is described throughout the rest of this book. WHAT you are measuring for is improved quality, increased customer satisfaction and increased profitability.

There you have it. These are some of the most important reasons WHY you must measure quality and customer satisfaction. Now, we are going to discuss HOW to do it. The research and measurement techniques associated with quality and customer satisfaction will be presented so that you do not have to be a statistician or an engineer to use them. In fact, I am neither, so I promise to present them in a manner everyone can understand.

TOOLS FOR MEASURING QUALITY

There are a variety of tools for measuring quality and customer satisfaction, and many of these can be used interchangeably. However, there is an accepted set of seven ''basic'' tools for measuring quality. These include:

- Check Sheets
- Pareto Charts
- Histograms
- Scatter Diagrams (Correlation Diagrams)
- Cause and Effect Diagrams (Fishbone Diagrams; Ishikawa Diagrams—the originator)
- Graph and Control (Run) Charts
- Stratification

There are other measurement techniques that can be used, such as brainstorming, nominal groups, flow charting (also known as blueprinting), force field analysis and benchmarking. Each will be described for you with an example of how it is used to measure quality and the relation to customer satisfaction.

Tool #1: Check Sheets

Check sheets are simply an easy way to understand how often certain poor-quality events, or instances of customer dissatisfaction and satisfaction, are occurring. A columnar form is developed that identifies the events being investigated along with the time period for investigation. Then, data is gathered within each of the event areas and tick marks are placed inside the time period column. A total column is used to summarize the entire measurement process.

Let's take an example of how often a company ships the wrong parts to a manufacturer. The first column would be a list of the possible events, including incorrect shipping, that could contribute to the manufacturer receiving the wrong parts. The next three columns identify the time period under investigation, such as three separate months. Finally, the total column tells you which problem area is most significant during the researched time period.

TOOL #1: CHECK SHEETS (continued)

This simple technique allows you to determine where your costs of poor quality are coming from, as well as your sources of customer dissatisfaction.

The chart below illustrates a check sheet for this problem

Problem	Month 1	Month 2	Month 3	TOTALS
Order Entry Error	////	//	/	7
Stock Selection Error	///	////	////	11
Orders Mixed Up	///	///	///	9
Wrong Order Shipped	0	////	////	8

Based on the data collected in this check sheet, we can assume that the manufacturer receives the wrong parts from the supplier due to stock selection errors. Obviously, since the manufacturer cannot produce the products his customer wants, there are now two dissatisfied customers: the manufacturer, who is a customer of the supplier, and the end user of the finished product, who is a customer of the manufacturer.

If the check sheet measurement technique resembles a frequency distribution from your basic statistics course, you are right. Sometimes, the most effective measurements, at least to get you started, are the simplest.

Tool #2: Pareto Charts

A Pareto Chart is a vertical bar graph that helps you identify problems in quality and customer satisfaction by the frequency of their occurrence. The graphic representation also helps you determine which problems to solve and in what order. With a Pareto Chart, you can easily see how seemingly small problems can cause bigger problems, and how these may require your utmost attention. The Pareto Chart is based on data-collection methods such as the check sheet, frequency distribution or participant observation.

To construct a Pareto Chart, you must first identify the problems to be studied then decide on a unit of measurement. Collect the data over a specified period of time, and then draw your results on a graph in priority order with the most frequently occurring problem being drawn first (it will have the tallest bar in the graph) and the other problems depicted in descending order. The chart will provide you with an analysis of how a small percentage of activities (typically 20%) causes a much larger percentage (typically 80%) of the quality problems. Hence, the Pareto Principle is also called the 80/20 rule, and the chart illustrates this visually.

If we use the data in the check sheet from the previous page, we have four problem areas: order-entry problems, stock-selection errors, orders from different companies being mixes up, and the wrong parts (orders) being shipped. To develop the Pareto Chart, we simply graph the events in descending order of their occurrence. This means that the first bar represents stock-selection errors; the second bar is for mixing up orders; the third bar is for actually shipping the wrong orders; and the fourth bar is for order-entry problems.

With this Pareto Chart, we now know that the first thing we have to work on is stock-selection errors followed by more accurate tracking of orders per company. Without the chart, we may have decided that order entry was our main problem and spent a great deal of time trying to correct the least-important problem area.

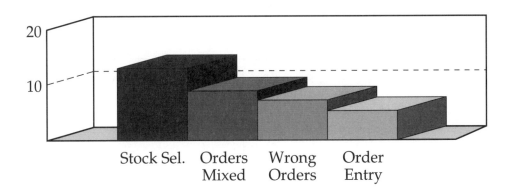

Tool #3: Histograms

Histograms are also vertical bar graphs, similar to the Pareto Chart with one basic difference. Histograms display numerical information about the frequency of distribution of continuous data, whereas the Pareto Chart illustrates characteristics of a product, process or service. For example, if you were trying to graphically illustrate how many of your employees take a certain number of sick days per year, you would collect data on sick time in a check sheet format. Then, you would create a range for your data, which is simply the difference between the least number of days taken off and the most. Then, decide on how many intervals (columns on the bar graph) you want to show your data. Divide the number of intervals into the range to determine how large each interval will be. The number of intervals determines the size of the intervals and how many occurrences will fall within each. Next, decide on the scale you will use for the vertical axis (Y axis), and then once you have drawn the histogram, calculate the measures of central tendency:

- Mean: the average of all the sick days, which is the total number of sick days divided by the number of employees.

- Median: the midpoint of the distribution of the data. This is the point where 50% of all the data fall above and below on the graph.

- Mode: the most commonly observed number of sick days, or interval.

You can then complete the histogram by adding the names of the measures of central tendency to the graph. The table below is a frequency distribution for employees taking sick days, followed by the histogram representing the data.

NUMBER OF SICK DAYS PER YEAR	NUMBER OF EMPLOYEES
1	2
2	3
3	6
4	10
5	7
6	8
7	5
8	8
Total 248	**Total 49**

The total number of employees taking sick days equals 49. The total number of sick days taken equals 248. The average number of sick days per employee is 5.06. The mode of the distribution is 4 sick days, as that is the number that comes up most often. The median point is between 4 and 5 days. The histogram looks like this. It will have 4 bars with an interval of two days each (range of 8 divided by 4 bars).

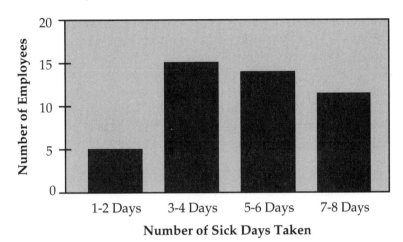

Histograms provide you with a tremendous amount of information, based on the shape of the graph. If most of the numbers and bars are in the center of the graph, then there is a small variation in your quality process. If the bars are spread out along the horizontal X axis, then there is a large variability in your quality process. When most of the numbers are toward the left of the graph, there is a positive skew to the histogram. Conversely, if most of the bars are to the right of the graph, there is a negative skew to the diagram. Finally, if you have two peaks in your histogram, you have variations in your quality process coming from two sources and you must investigate this immediately.

Tool #4: Scatter Diagrams (Correlation Diagrams)

Scatter diagrams are used to study the potential relationship between two variables. This diagram is used to test for possible correlational relationships. If a relationship exists, you will see a change in one variable as soon as there is a change in the second variable.

To create a scatter diagram, identify the two variables you want to study. Label the X axis with one of the variable names and the Y axis with the other. The variable that is being investigated as the possible cause of the relationship is usually placed on the X (horizontal) axis.

Collect the data and plot each data point. View the diagram and see how the points cluster or "scatter" throughout the graph. The closer the points are to resembling a straight line, the stronger the correlation is between these two variables. Look for positive, negative or nonrelationships.

A positive relationship occurs when Y increases as X increases: the graph goes from the lower left to the upper right. A negative relationship occurs when X decreases as Y increases: the graph goes from the upper left to the lower right. A nonrelationship occurs when the dots are scattered all over the graph.

When viewing a scatter diagram, you can only say that X and Y are related and not that one causes the other. You need more stringent statistical techniques to determine cause and effect, and you can find them in any statistics textbook.

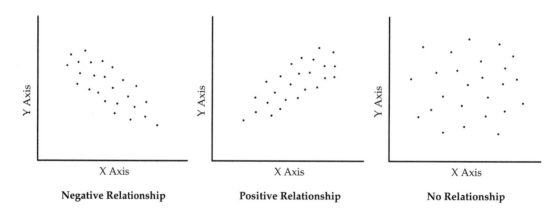

Examples of Relationships

Tool #5: Cause-and-Effect Diagrams

Cause-and-effect diagrams are also known as fishbone diagrams because of their appearance. The simplest of these diagrams takes a final effect and tries to determine causes by breaking the causes up into various categories. (See Figure 1a.) The standard categories (major causes) are manpower or people, machines or equipment, materials or supplies, and methods or processes. Each of these categories is placed on a bone or spine so that the entire diagram looks like the skeleton of a fish.

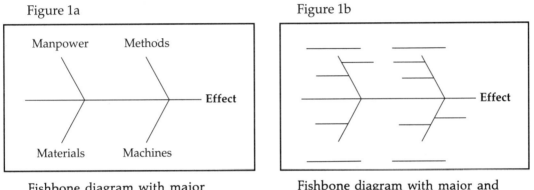

Figure 1a

Fishbone diagram with major causes and effect.

Figure 1b

Fishbone diagram with major and minor causes and effect.

Then, you begin to fill in the ''smaller bones'' (minor causes) on each potential major cause until you have identified what you believe to be *all* the possible causes of the effect. (See Figure 1b.) Remember that you do not have to limit yourself to these category headings. For example, in a service business the categories may be policies, procedures, people, and plant (the office or location). Your purpose is to identify all the possible causes and to determine if any relationships exist between the causes and the effect.

Once you have completed the fishbone diagram, you identify those causes you perceive to be the most important and subject them to further study. To make this decision, look for things that have changed dramatically, that deviate from the norm or that have atypical performance patterns. Then, identify how these are affecting the quality of your work and the level of your customers' satisfaction. You may even want to create a cause-and-effect diagram for the cause you have selected, thereby identifying the causes of the cause. Take this back as far as you find useful.

Use the cause-and-effect diagram above to identify one area that you think needs improvement, such as your response time to service requests, your handling of customer complaints or the methods you use to measure customer satisfaction. Fill in the fishbones and decide which cause needs further study. Then, undertake that study, find a solution and implement it.

Tool #6: Graph, Control and Run Charts

These are all visual representations of your measurement data. You are probably already familiar with a number of types of graphs: bar graphs (both vertical and horizontal), pie charts, line graphs and stacked bar graphs. Pareto Charts and Histograms are also types of graphs. A graph simply provides the viewer with a pictorial representation of the collected data.

A **run chart** is a line graph. It is a collection of data points (measurements) over a specified period of time that are plotted on a graph. You may also include a straight line on the run chart to represent the average of all the measurement data.

For example, let's assume you are trying to determine why customers are returning items they purchased from you. Returns can either be a measure of customer dissatisfaction or the customer's perception of a poor quality purchase. You must determine this with other methods. You want to use the run chart to measure the number of returns per day on an hourly basis, per week or per month. You decide on the measurement criteria and time period. Below is an example of what this run chart might look like for a seven-day period.

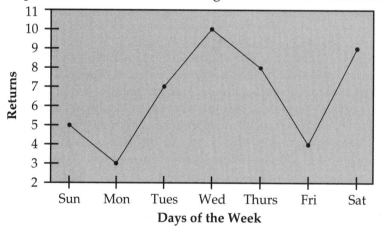

Your analysis of this chart reveals that the greatest number of returns occurs at midweek and at the end of the week. Now, you may want to use a fishbone diagram to determine what is causing returns at these times.

One other point about run charts. If you collect enough data, you would expect that an identical number of points would fall above and below the average line. If the points indicate an upward or downward trend, or a significant number of them are either above or below the average, then this is cause for further investigation.

A more sophisticated run chart is the **control chart,** which is simply a run chart with a statistically determined upper and lower limit. These limits are drawn on either side of the average line on the chart, and the run chart is superimposed on the control chart. The statistical calculation is simply + or − 3 standard deviations from the mean.

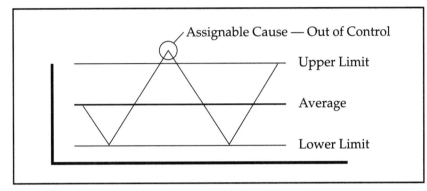

You should know several things about control charts. The first is that they identify limits within which a process or performance is consistent. It can be either consistently bad or consistently good. And, just because a process is within statistical limits does not mean the process is within specified limits, since the specified limits are determined by the customer. In other words, the customer's specified limits can be more stringent than the statistically defined control limits of the process.

Finally, the process or performance can be within statistical and specified limits, be consistent, and said to be in control. But, if it does not do what the customer wants it to do, it is not a quality product and the customer will not be satisfied.

Control charts help you determine quality but do nothing for determining the underlying causes of a process. (This must be determined with other techniques.) Also, control charts help you determine how variability occurs within the process. Variability can be either random (chance) or assignable. Chance variability is that which is expected to occur when a quality process runs within statistical control limits. Chance causes are always present, inherent in the nature of the process, cannot be identified or removed, and are impossible to control because of their unknown nature.

On the other hand, **assignable causes** are due to nonrandom variations. Assignable causes are unpredictable, identifiable, capable of being controlled, removable and require immediate attention and action. You know you have an assignable variation when your control chart shows data points that are outside the upper or lower limits.

42

Tool #7: Stratification

Stratification is simply a method to become more accurate in the collection and reporting of your measurement data. There may be times when the data itself masks the actual individual sources of that data. For example, the run chart depicting the number of returns "lumps" all the returned items together. However, you would probably want to know which items were returned the most. That is where stratification comes in.

Break up the data into discrete categories, such as type, location, size, department, distance and so forth. This allows you to determine more clearly and precisely your areas for quality improvement.

As an example, consider your measurements of customer satisfaction. Let's say that you determine that 70% of your customers are satisfied with your product or service and 30% are dissatisfied. This is a general figure. It would be to your benefit to know more about both groups. One way to do this is to stratify them by demographics: age, gender, income, zip code and so on. Then, you would have a more accurate picture of your customers and their responses.

The results of your stratification process can be drawn as a Pareto Chart, a Histogram or a run chart. Use whatever method you feel most comfortable with.

These are the seven basic tools for measuring quality in a business. Each has its place in measuring quality and can also be used to measure customer satisfaction after you have gathered your satisfaction data. Also, the charting techniques of quality improvement are excellent graphics for depicting levels of customer satisfaction.

There are more sophisticated statistical analysis techniques that can be used to measure quality, but they are beyond the scope of this book. Refer to statistics texts or contact the American Society for Quality Control at 800-248-1946 for other references.

OTHER MEASUREMENT TECHNIQUES

Benchmarking

Benchmarking is a technique where you compare your procedures in a given area to another company that is considered to be the best in that class. This other company does not necessarily have to be in your industry. However, you can benchmark directly against your major competitor.

The simplest way to benchmark is to determine exactly what your customers want that you may not be giving them. Then, identify the company that is the "best in its class" in providing that service. Contact it directly to learn how it does it, then copy and adapt these efforts. Measure what you do to determine how effective your benchmarking has been.

Brainstorming

This is not so much a measurement technique as it is a way to generate creative ideas for continuous quality improvement. Brainstorming is usually broken down into three phases. Phase 1 is concerned with the quantity of ideas that your group can generate. Phase 2 requires a review of the ideas and an elimination of those ideas that do not point you toward your goal. Phase 3 involves further review and a prioritization of the remaining ideas in the order the group believes will help the company achieve its quality goal.

The rules of brainstorming are very simple. Select a person to record all the ideas on a flip chart or board. Then, each person in the group calls out an idea related or unrelated to the topic at hand. No one makes an evaluation or a critical judgment of any of the ideas during this initial phase. When all related ideas are exhausted, then the group can begin with unrelated ideas. When creativity seems to be at its end, then the group reviews the list and eliminates those ideas that do not seem relevant. Finally, the group makes a final list and prioritizes it.

The critical components of brainstorming are: all ideas are valid; no judgments are made; each person can link or build on the previous idea; no ideas can be criticized; and all ideas are initially accepted.

BRAINSTORMING (continued)

Brainstorming can also be done by an individual. Think of several areas in your company or business field that can be improved. In the space below, write down all the quality improvement ideas you can think of within five minutes. Then, repeat the exercise with three or four other coworkers and see how many ideas you can generate.

_____

_____

_____

_____

_____

_____

_____

_____

_____

_____

A more highly structured form of brainstorming is the **nominal group technique** (NGT). With NGT, you present an idea or topic to the group, preferably in the form of a question. Then, each member of the group individually records as many of his or her ideas in response to the question as possible. Then, each person mentions one idea at a time and the recorder writes it on the board. An idea can only be recorded once. After all the ideas have been presented, the group members write down the entire list and then prioritize the items. These rank orders are collected by the recorder and added. The idea with the highest cumulative total is selected as the most important one and subjected to further analysis. This process continues for all prioritized items.

The advantages of this technique are that you create a rank order for many quality-improvement and customer-satisfaction ideas, and each member of the group contributes equally into determining the whole group's priorities.

Force Field Analysis

This is another technique that helps more with understanding quality than measuring it. With force field analysis, you are trying to understand the forces that **drive** you toward quality improvement and those that **restrain** you from achieving it in a given situation. If restraining forces are stronger or more numerous than driving forces, then quality improvement will probably not take place.

You use force field analysis to identify how a current process works and how it can be improved. This analysis will also help you determine how to over-come the restraining forces and encourage any changes in interpersonal or organizational behavior that are necessary.

Here is an example of a force field analysis for improving the quality of a customer service operation that responds to callers' inquiries for software technical support.

DRIVING FORCES	RESTRAINING FORCES
Quicker response reduces complaints →	← Need more staff
More referrals →	← Increased training
Increased profits →	← Greater accountability
More satisfied customers →	← May need to raise product costs

Now, create your own force field analysis for a quality-improvement opportunity in your business.

DRIVING FORCES	RESTRAINING FORCES

Flowcharting

Flowcharting, also known as blueprinting, helps you graphically depict and describe a process as it occurs. You may know these as decision trees or algorithms.

Flowcharting helps you break a process down step by step to determine what is done when, where and by whom, and how each behavior occurs at a specific decision point. This is a very effective technique to identify gaps in quality-service and customer-satisfaction efforts.

Flowcharting uses six basic symbols to denote a particular step or action within an improvement process.

Symbol		Denotes	Examples
Circle	○	Operation	Calling, typing, filing
Square	□	Inspection	Check, review, measure
Arrow	→	Transport	Moving things
Diamond	◇	Decision	Determine what to do
"Large" D	D	Delay	Waiting for work, wait in line
Triangle	△	Filing/Storage	Data entry

Using these six basic symbols, you can develop a flow chart or blueprint for every activity that occurs in your company. Think, for a minute, about a particular process that heavily affects customer satisfaction. Now, draw a flow chart of that entire process. You will have to take your time to think about all the steps that occur as well as the possible pitfalls in the process. However, when you have completed the flow chart, you will have an ideal way to determine how you can now improve your service quality and subsequently increase your level of customer satisfaction.

THE WHY AND HOW OF QUALITY IMPROVEMENT AND CUSTOMER SATISFACTION

There are two other investigative techniques you must implement to improve your quality and levels of customer satisfaction. They are known as the ''5-Why's'' and the ''5-How's,'' and are also called root cause analysis.

All you do is continue to ask successive questions of why and how related to a specific topic. It is recommended that you ask these questions at least 5 times, although some people have found great success with 7 or 10 levels of questions.

Here is an example related to improving customer satisfaction.

1. Why are customers dissatisfied?

   Anwser: Because they are not receiving their purchases on time.

2. Why are they not receiving their purchases on time?

   Answer: Because we are backordered on stock.

3. Why are we backordered on stock?

   Answer: Because we changed suppliers.

4. Why did we change suppliers?

   Answer: Because the original supplier was late with shipments.

5. Why haven't we found another supplier?

   Answer: Because we have not yet looked for one. (and so on)

The root cause of this problem lies with the supplier, and the company must change suppliers to prevent customer dissatisfaction.

This particular line of questioning leads one to conclude that customer satisfaction in this instance is related to a) shipping customer orders on time, and b) receiving the stock from suppliers in a timely manner. The company, or the person asking the ''why'' questions, can now identify areas for improvement that will ultimately lead to increased customer satisfaction.

THE WHY AND HOW OF QUALITY IMPROVEMENT AND CUSTOMER SATISFACTION (continued)

The same approach holds true with the ''how'' questions.

1. How can we improve customer satisfaction?

Answer: By making sure orders are shipped on time.

2. How can we make sure we ship orders on time?

Answer: By informing suppliers of our demand.

3. How can we better communicate our needs to our suppliers?

Answer: By reviewing our past history in ordering and receiving shipments.

4. How can we collect this information?

Answer: By checking with our purchasing department.

5. How can we get purchasing to help us increase our levels of customer satisfaction?

Answer: By showing them how their work affects suppliers and customers.

In this ''how'' example, you see *how* external customer satisfaction is impacted by internal purchasing behaviors. If you did not question yourself to this level of detail, you may have only dealt with external features of customer contact or developed programs for your frontline employees.

The ''WHY'' and ''HOW'' questioning techniques focus more on problem solving and information gathering than measurement. They are invaluable in helping you identify goals and objectives. In fact, one of my clients facetiously called them ''stupid questions,'' because they were so simple, his staff had never thought to ask or answer them.

ONE LAST THOUGHT ABOUT MEASURING QUALITY

There is one more thing that must be mentioned about measuring quality, service quality, and quality improvement. All of the measuring techniques, whether they are idea-generators such as brainstorming, NGT, force field analysis or flowcharting, or they are actual statistical tools, such as check sheets, histograms, Pareto diagrams, scatter diagrams, run charts, control charts or stratification, have one thing in common. *They are basically internal measurement tools and techniques.*

They are important, and they do give you a clear and concise picture of how well your company is providing a quality product or service. However, *quality is only what the customer defines it to be.* Sometimes, the customer cannot even describe what quality is, but they know it when they see it (or hear or feel it). Therefore, you must consider your internal quality measurements in the proper perspective. That is, your product or service can meet all of your internal requirements and still not perform the way the customer wants it to. The customer is not satisfied. Therefore, from a business mindset, you have not provided a quality product or service.

Keep this in mind every time you measure your quality. Your internal measurements are important, but they become meaningless if the customers are not satisfied with what you give them. In order to make your quality measurements more meaningful and more appropriate, ASK your customers what they want from you. Find out exactly what will satisfy them, and create and measure your products and services accordingly.

P A R T

III

Researching Customer Satisfaction

RESEARCH METHODS

Measures of quality are internal to your company or organization. Now, you must go outside your company's boundaries and measure the satisfaction levels of your customers. You do this through a variety of research methods and data-collection techniques.

Secondary Data

Secondary data is information that has been collected for some other purpose than the one you are currently investigating. Sources of secondary data include information you already have within your company as well as information you can get from stock reports, trade publications, research organizations, census data and any other providers of information.

For example, if you are interested in what type of customers in your industry buy the most of your product or register the most complaints, you may ask your trade association for information on purchaser characteristics or profiles of complaining customers. This information may be available through warranty information or from research conducted for some other reason and the trade association just happens to be able to provide it for you. That is secondary data. You have not collected it yourself to research a particular problem or situation.

The advantages of secondary data are that they provide both cost and time economies. The information is already available and it is usually free, especially if you check your local library. The disadvantages are that the data may not directly fit your customer satisfaction situation, the data may be obsolete by the time you use it, and also, it may not be accurate enough for you to make informed decisions about customer service.

Again, consider your secondary data with care as you relate it to customer satisfaction levels. However, when you begin to measure customer satisfaction levels, always use secondary data as it can help you develop a better focus on your primary data-collection methods.

RESEARCH METHODS (continued)

Primary Data

Primary data is information you collect yourself that is directly related to your research project, in this case, measures of customer satisfaction. While primary data collection is much more accurate because it relates specifically to the customer research you are conducting, it is also much more expensive. You collect primary data through a number of means, including but not limited to experiments, surveys, questionnaires, interviews, and opinion polls. You also use primary data to determine peoples' attitudes, opinions, preferences, behaviors and personalities.

Primary data collection can be used to classify your current customers into demographic, psychographic and sociographic categories. This helps you to more accurately determine the profile of the people responding to your inquiries. For example, if you know that your male customers with incomes over $35,000.00 make more purchases of your product or service than female customers in the same income bracket, you can target your marketing efforts in this direction. You can also determine the satisfaction levels of both groups, and if the female group is less satisfied, you can conduct additional research to learn these reasons and then develop programs, products or services to increase the satisfaction level of this customer group.

Write down your current sources of secondary and primary data in the chart below.

Secondary	Primary

You collect primary data either through communication or observation techniques. Communication means surveys and interviews requiring direct involvement of the customer, and observation means simply watching the customers' behaviors. Both of these techniques are valid as you try to measure your customers' satisfaction levels.

Qualitative Research

Qualitative research attempts to subjectively understand the experience of the customer when they purchase or use your product or service. There are no hard measurements with qualitative research. You collect information on customer satisfaction levels through observation, interviews, focus groups and personal experience (where you act as your own customer).

Even though it is difficult to quantify this type of information, you can gain tremendous insight into what your customers think about your quality and service. Usually, customers will be more than happy to tell you their perceptions, thoughts and feelings about your product or service. You must then compile and collate this information so that you can use it to determine ways to improve your service quality and customer satisfaction ratings.

Quantitative Research

Quantitative research is objective and measurable. You collect information according to some predetermined standard, such as a five- or seven-point scale, using a questionnaire, or survey. This survey can be written, oral or conducted over the telephone. When you have completed your research, you perform statistical analyses on the data to determine your customer satisfaction ratings and your customers' ratings of your service quality.

RESEARCH METHODS (continued)

Sampling

Sampling is a determination of how many customers you will research in order to get the information you are seeking. There is no ideal sample size for a given research project, unless of course you can survey or interview every customer you do business with. Unfortunately, this is not practical or feasible, so you must research a representative sample. Statistics books will tell you how to determine the exact sample size for your project. For most purposes, if you can research 50–100 people (or more) at a given time, you probably have a representative sample.

You can increase the power of your research and sample by randomly selecting the customers you want to survey or interview. Random selection means just what it says. You pick the people at random without any predetermining factors. Again, for more information, consult a research methods or statistics book.

Research Design: An Example

Here is an example of a customer-satisfaction research project. It is elegant in its simplicity yet it is extremely effective in gathering the information a company would need. Follow it, and then fill in the chart to design your own satisfaction research project.

Category	Description
Objective	To determine customer-satisfaction levels of training programs
Time Period	July–December, 1992
Sample	All purchasers, male and female: minimum 100 subjects
Format	Written survey with scaled responses
Analysis	Percentages, histograms and Pareto charts
Data Collection Time	January, 1993
Report	Distributed to all employees
Follow up	Work to improve areas of service quality that need attention as determined by the survey

Now, fill in your descriptors of the category. This brief outline will give you a format to follow when conducting your customer satisfaction research. Also, notice how quality improvement tools (histogram, Pareto chart) can be used to describe satisfaction measurement results.

Category	Description
Objective	
Time Period	
Sample	
Format	
Analysis	
Data Collection Time	
Report	
Follow up	

You now have a basic background in research methods. You are ready to develop your customer satisfaction research tools. How many of them are you familiar with? Check those that you know about and are confident you can use immediately. Review them in the following section and study those that you are unfamiliar with in greater depth.

DATA COLLECTION TECHNIQUES

I am familiar with the following data collection techniques:

- ☐ Questionnaires
- ☐ Surveys (written)
- ☐ Telephone Surveys
- ☐ Focus Groups
- ☐ Interviews (scheduled and personal; written or oral)
- ☐ Intercepts (a type of personal interview)

I am familiar with the following customer satisfaction reporting techniques:

- ☐ Customer Satisfaction Index or Rating
- ☐ Service Quality Measurement System
- ☐ Customer Report Card
- ☐ Service Standards of Performance
- ☐ Customer Satisfaction Benchmarking
- ☐ Attribute Ratings and Perceptual Maps

These are the most common customer satisfaction measurement tools and techniques. Move on to the next section to learn what they are and how to use them.

EXPLANATIONS

QUESTIONNAIRES AND SURVEYS

Most customer satisfaction measurements are taken by surveys. These can be written or oral questionnaires, telephone or face-to-face interviews, and focus groups. An intercept measurement is simply when a researcher stops a customer as they enter or leave a place of business and begins to ask them questions. The customer is "intercepted." The intercept technique can be either a written survey or oral interview or both.

The survey method is by far the most common data collection technique. Surveys usually consist of several questions or statements along with associated responses that require people to answer according to some predefined scale. Some surveys allow people to answer in an open-ended manner, thereby describing their responses in greater detail. Both response methods are useful and provide excellent information about customer satisfaction levels.

Surveys are typically self-report mechanisms where the customer answers the questions for himself or herself. Sometimes, other people respond for the customer. In either case, the idea is to get the customer to provide the most accurate answers to your questions so that you can evaluate your service quality, customer service efforts, and levels of customer satisfaction.

Format and Layout

There are numerous formats and layouts you can use for your surveys, and several are shown in the Appendix. The key is to keep the survey "user friendly," easy to understand and respond to. Also, don't make the survey too long, as people will begin to lose interest in an extensive survey, especially if you have "intercepted" them to get their responses.

If you mail out the survey to your customers, you have a better chance of them completing a lengthy questionnaire than if you stop them in person. People perceive they have more time at home or at the office and, if they are interested in your business, will take the time to complete your survey.

QUESTIONNAIRES AND SURVEYS
(continued)

When you develop the survey, format it so the questions that are easiest to answer are at the beginning. This gives the customer a feeling of accomplishment and a sense of comfort with the survey. Sometimes, these first few ''giveaway'' questions are simple, open-ended questions that get the respondent into writing and thinking about the survey. Here are three questions you can use or modify at the beginning of your survey.

1. What reason did you have for shopping with us today?

2. Have you purchased from us before?

3. Did you find everything you were looking for?

These are simple, open-ended and yes/no questions that get the customer into the habit of responding. You must also consider the format and layout. Do you want the questions to be followed by the answers on the same line with a leader (. . . .) to the answers? Or, do you want the answers placed below the questions? The choice is yours. Here is what both formats look like. Surveys have been successful at obtaining information using both formats.

---

1. How satisfied were you with the service you received from our staff . . . .

	Dissatisfied		Somewhat		Very Satisfied
	1	2	3	4	5

OR,

1. How satisfied were you with the service you received from our staff?

Dissatisfied	Somewhat	Very Satisfied
1	2	3

You must decide which format and layout works best for you and your customers. You may want to test both and determine which surveys with a particular format receive more responses and returns.

Question Construction

One of the keys to a successful survey is that the questions actually ask what they are supposed to be asking. Also, there should be only one thought or attribute or skill being rated per question. For example, asking a customer ''Was the staff courteous and friendly?'' does not give you any information you can use. What are you trying to get at: courtesy or friendliness? And, when they answer yes or no, which one are they responding to: courtesy or friendliness? If you are trying to find out about either courtesy or friendliness, or both, ask separate questions for each.

Your most important ingredient constructing survey questions is to make sure the questions are simple and direct with only one thought or item per question. Then, ask enough questions on your survey to get all the information you want from your customers and to be able to determine their level of satisfaction with you.

QUESTIONNAIRES AND SURVEYS (continued)

Survey Question Responses

Responses to questions are either open ended or closed ended, the latter usually being a rating of some kind. When you look at a survey, you can immediately tell the response being called for by the start of the question or statement. If it begins with What, Where, Who, Why, Describe, Tell or List, it is an open-ended question requiring a descriptive or subjective answer. If the question begins with Did or Were or a pronoun, it is usually a closed-ended response that is required. There are times when questions or statements can begin with any of these words and be the opposite of the norm. However, the majority of the time, these classifications hold true.

Since we want to measure customer satisfaction, we need "hard" data, and that comes from measurements. Therefore, you should scale your responses to each question, and try to use the same scale whenever and wherever possible within the same survey.

Scales can be ordinal, where the answer ranges from "Poor to Excellent," with one, two or three other possible responses in between. This is acceptable. Unfortunately, when we use these scales, we then put numbers on them, such as 1 through 5, and then analyze those numbers. Ordinal data do not have true numerical intervals and should not be analyzed in this way. However, most managers tend to do this and it has become accepted practice among customer service researchers to analyze this type of data as if it were truly numerical. So, if you are measuring your satisfaction levels using category descriptions and then converting them to numbers, go ahead, even if research and statistical purists will cringe.

Your scales should always contain an odd number of possible responses, such as 3, 5, or 7. This allows a neutral point for the respondent. When you are working with percentages, you may want to use a 10 or 100 point scale. This is fine as long as you don't mix the analysis of the scales, even if you do mix the use of different types of scales in the same survey.

Here are the most widely used types of scales in customer-satisfaction measurement.

3 POINT SCALE

1	2	3
Poor	Fair	Excellent

4 POINT SCALE (used but not highly recommended)

1	2	3	4
Worse	Somewhat Better	Better	Much Better

5 POINT SCALE

1	2	3	4	5
Poor	Fair	Neutral	Good	Excellent
(Well Below Expectations)	(Below Expectations)	(Meets Expectations)	(Above Expectations)	(Far Exceeds Expectations)

7 POINT SCALE (also known as Likert-type scale)

1	2	3	4	5	6	7
Very Poor (Dissatisfied)	Poor	Somewhat Poor	Neutral	Somewhat Good	Good	Very Good (Satisfied)

10 POINT SCALE (Add a 0 point to make it an 11 point scale)

1   2   3   4   5   6   7   8   9   10
Not   Extremely
At All   Important
Important

100 (101) POINT SCALE

0% ———————————————————— 100%
Complete   Complete
Dissatisfaction   Satisfaction

Note: For any of the rating scales and their descriptive terms, you can substitute satisfied and dissatisfied for the responses, or some wording about meeting, not meeting and exceeding expectations. Word your questions so the responses make sense to the customer.

Questionnaire and Survey Construction Checklist

Have you included or considered the following in developing your survey?

- ☐ Format and Layout
- ☐ Question Construction (one item per question)
- ☐ Response Requirements (open or closed ended, forced choice or paired comparisons)
- ☐ Types of Scales for Responses
- ☐ Data Analysis Techniques (based on questions and response types)
- ☐ Reporting Requirements and Mechanisms (who receives the final information)

Make It Easy On Yourself

As a consultant specializing in customer satisfaction and service quality, I help clients do a great deal of research and measurement into the satisfaction levels of their customers. This requires developing surveys of various types and lengths for different clients in different industries. In the past, we used to have a printer typeset and print the survey. Then, when we received the responses, they were input into a database or spreadsheet program for analysis and reporting. Now, there is an easier way.

Survey Pro, a software program from Apian Software, helps you design, format, layout and select responses for your customer-satisfaction surveys. Then, when it comes time to analyze your response data, you just go back into Survey Pro's analysis module, input your responses, and then ask the program for whatever statistical reports you desire. You can do cross tabulations, compare two or more variables, and you can even do more sophisticated analyses. I have no financial stake in Apian Software, and I must tell you that it has made my life much easier with all that it can do.

It is a program that is totally dedicated to survey construction and response analysis. Apian Software can be reached at PO Box 1224, Menlo Park, California 94026 or by calling (800) 237-4565. Survey Pro is available in both DOS and Windows versions. An example of a survey developed and printed by Survey Pro is in the Appendix. Also, an audio program with a comprehensive workbook developed by the Institute for International Research called Measuring and Improving Customer Satisfaction will be helpful to you. It describes how various companies in different industries have developed and implemented their customer satisfaction measurement program. The Institute can be reached at 437 Madison Ave., 23rd Floor, New York, N.Y. 10022 or by calling (800) 999-3123.

TELEPHONE SURVEYS

Telephone surveys are very effective in gathering customer-satisfaction data if the surveyor is well trained in asking the survey questions, there is a script to follow, and the customer is not called at an inconvenient time. The advantage of telephone surveys over written (mailed) surveys and questionnaires is that an experienced surveyor (customer service representative or telemarketer) can focus on what the respondent is saying and gear open-ended questions to particular responses and elicit more information. Plus, the surveyor can make determinations from the respondent's tone of voice regarding the veracity of the answers. The main disadvantage of telephone surveys is that the respondent can hang up on you at any time, or may never even talk to you. Also, you are not always able to get someone at home or the office to interview them.

In either case, telephone surveys are an excellent tool to support written surveys, and in appropriate instances, they can be used as your sole data-collection technique.

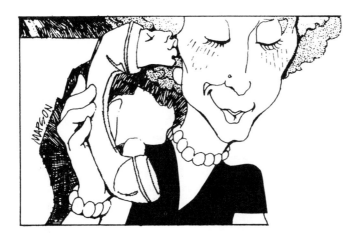

Using Telephone Surveys Successfully

Follow these five basic principles for telephone survey success.

1. Keep the survey simple

Since the respondent is listening to the questions or statements, make them and the response scales easy to understand. Complex questions, multiple answers or response scales have no place in a telephone customer-satisfaction survey. Show appreciation for customers who have agreed to help you out by responding to your telephone inquiry by not taking too much of their time or confusing them.

2. Have a script

Give all your telephone surveyors a script to follow. The script should contain information about how they introduce themselves when the customer answers the phone, how they ask each question, how they respond to customer questions, what to do when a customer goes off on a tangent with an answer, how to keep a customer on the line to complete the survey and how to thank the customer for helping you. Make sure everyone follows the script to the letter. This is not a telemarketing sales script. It is a customer-research script and you must always do everything the same way in order to preserve the integrity of the data.

3. Make the response form easy to work with

Your surveyors must be able to record a customer's response to a question very quickly and then be able to move on to the next question. The response form must be easy for them to work with and follow so that they never place a response in the wrong column or next to a different question than the one for which it was intended.

The format and layout for your telephone surveys should have the question along the top and the responses flush right in a column. This will minimize, and hopefully negate, any possibility of a mistake on your surveyor's part. Here is an example of the telephone interview survey and response form.

---

1. How satisfied were you with the service you received from the front desk staff?

Very Dissatisfied	1
Somewhat Dissatisfied	2
It was O.K.	3
Somewhat Satisfied	4
Very Satisfied	5

Your telephone surveyor simply circles the response the customer gives, and since the responses are "way off to the right," there should be no cause for confusion or problems. One thing you should try to do with your telephone survey is to keep the response key or scales the same for each question, and this holds true for written surveys as well. While it is true you can provide new instructions to the respondent, or on a written survey the person can read the instructions related to the new response scales, it is easier for everyone if you use one scale throughout the survey.

Again, remember that there is no true right or wrong here. What I am advocating is elegant simplicity, especially if you have minimal experience with customer-satisfaction surveys and research.

4. Train your surveyors

This alone will make or break your telephone survey. The survey can be great, properly worded, easy to use with an excellent response form; the script can be simple to follow, and the customer can be ready to respond. However, if your surveyors are not trained in how to communicate and administer the survey as well as record the responses, there will definitely be problems. Train them extensively, and don't let them call a customer until you are satisfied that they have interviewed you appropriately.

5. Thank the customer

This may seem a little ironic or out of place to be included in steps to making a telephone survey successful. On the contrary, saying thank you at the beginning when the customer agrees to the survey, saying thank you during the survey after every few questions, and definitely saying thank you upon the completion of the survey will make your data collection easier, more effective, and give you a more accurate picture of how well you are satisfying your customers. Customers who perceive you care about them and trust you will be more likely to give you honest answers.

Analyzing the Telephone Survey

After all the data has been collected, you conduct the same types of statistical analyses on the telephone survey data as you would on written survey responses. You can also combine the results of telephone and written surveys and then subject them to analysis. An interesting point may be to classify the responses according to how the data were collected to see if there are any differences in your customers' levels of satisfaction based on whether they responded in writing (self-report) or by telephone.

Something to Think About

Telephone surveys, just like face-to-face interviews, are going to require a time investment on the part of the customer. Therefore, you may want to think about scheduling a telephone interview appointment with the customer, just as you would if you were going to interview the customer in person. You may find that the customer is much more appreciative and receptive to you since you are showing a concern for his or her valuable time. Plus, you may get more information from the customer than you were looking for in the survey. Think about how you feel when your telephone rings at dinner time and someone wants to ask you just a few questions. Telephone survey appointments will not always get a customer to agree to respond to you, but you should consider this option.

PERSONAL INTERVIEWS

Personal interviews can be either structured or unstructured. Structured interviews require you to ask specific questions of your customer in a particular order. You attempt not to deviate, and if the customer goes off on a tangent, you try to bring him or her back to the issue at hand.

If you have never conducted a structured customer-satisfaction interview, you should first develop a script describing the introduction and purpose of the interview, instructions for how you will ask questions and the scale of response they should consider when answering, and then have a list of questions and their related or expected responses. If the customers will be allowed to answer in a qualitative or subjective manner, you must tell them that at the beginning. When the customer answers your question, you mark the response directly on your form. If the answer is not one that you expected, you write it down as close to verbatim as possible. You may even want to record the session to make sure you do not miss any important information.

Unstructured interviews are highly subjective in nature and the customer is allowed to respond in almost a free associative manner. You ask certain questions, and then you see where the interview goes. Of course, you can ask specific questions during the unstructured interview as you would in a structured one, and I recommend it. However you do it, you must be able to record the customer's responses. If you are not a fast writer, then you should definitely record the interview, either on audio or video tape.

Another excellent use for the personal interview is to validate the written or telephone surveys. After you have received these responses, call some of the customers and invite them in for a personal interview. Speak with them one on one and try to identify an even deeper level of their feelings related to customer satisfaction. Again, record their responses and never forget to say thank you.

You may want to interview several people at one time. That is fine, and it brings us to the concept of focus groups.

FOCUS GROUPS

Focus groups are groups of people (customers), usually 5 to 10, who meet with a facilitator to answer questions related to a company's performance and to describe their satisfaction with the company's products or services. Focus groups are used extensively in market research but you have to remember that their value is in some ways limited to the specific group of respondents in attendance. Therefore, to validate your focus group information, conduct several different groups with customers from different parts of the country, with different purchasing habits, and who have different perceptions about your service quality and their level of satisfaction.

A focus group should be run by an outside facilitator who has experience in administering these types of group interviews. If you lead them yourselves, there is a tendency to bias the responses. So, invest the money and have someone from the outside help you. You will be more confident in your results when the facilitator has no stake in them.

Record the focus group, at least on audio tape if not both audio and video. Play it back several times to gather pieces of information you may have missed. Then, prepare a report on the comments and thoughts of the participants.

Although focus groups tend to be more subjective and open ended than written surveys, you can ask the customers to respond to specific questions with scaled response items. This will allow you to compare their responses directly with those you receive on the surveys.

Be careful of the "beneficent respondent" in your focus group. This is the person who will always give the answers he or she thinks you want to hear. While it may be a boost to your ego and a pat on your company's back to hear you are doing such a great job in satisfying your customers, this may actually be false information. Compare this person's responses with the rest of the focus group and against any written surveys you may have. Also, if this person has completed a written survey, or if you think the person may be a beneficent respondent, ask him or her to complete a survey, then compare the written responses with the oral ones. If they match, you have to dig further for the truth. If they don't match, you probably have a bias in your focus group data.

One other thing about focus groups. I have noticed that people are sometimes hesitant to participate in a "focus group," but they are very willing to be part of a "Customer Advisory Forum" or a "Customer Council." You can call it whatever you like. Determine which name your customers feel most comfortable with, call the group by that name, and you may be able to increase participation in the focus group for your customer-satisfaction research program.

REPORTING TECHNIQUES

Customer Satisfaction Index (CSI)

It can become very difficult for you to keep track of all the customer service, quality and satisfaction data you collect. Therefore, you probably will find it easier to develop a Customer Satisfaction Index (or Rating). This index is usually a compilation of all your scores into one number or percentage. For example, if you have customers rate you on 50 items or factors related to their satisfaction, you can take an average of all those scores and call it your index. Or, you can weight the responses according to importance and then create an index from the weighted scores. However you do it, remember that the Customer Satisfaction Index is not each individual rating but an average or compilation of many ratings.

Service Quality Measurement System (SQMS)

Your Service Quality Measurement System is the entire collection of tools and techniques you use to gather data and information about how well you are satisfying your customers. These tools can be any or all of the ones mentioned above plus mystery shoppers or simple comment cards (which are actually mini-surveys). Like the CSI mentioned above, the system is not a panacea for your customer service problems and improvement projects. The system alerts you to areas the customers think are important and then you must develop and implement programs to improve your services in those areas. Remember that you must ask the customers again about your improvements to determine if they are satisfied after you have made changes.

A problem with a SQMS is that it sometimes does not measure the types of service the customer expects in order to be satisfied. This occurs when a company makes up the entire system without asking and listening to the customer. Before you prepare your satisfaction measurement tools and techniques, speak with your customers and find out how they define quality, customer service, customer satisfaction and anything else they can evaluate you on. Then, devise the SQMS to measure these things.

Customer Report Card

This is a simple approach to quickly determine how customers feel about certain attributes related to the service you are providing. Many companies use a comment card to serve as a report card.

You develop the customer report card by first asking customers what attributes of your service they consider when they are determining quality and satisfaction levels. You then place them on a comment card and ask the customers to rate them according to some scale. You analyze the scores and data from these brief surveys the same way you would from more extensive surveys. An advantage of a customer report card is that it is short, easy to fill out and easy to score. Your report card rating can be a numerical tool of all the ratings made by the customers or a letter grade assigned to specific numerical ratings, much like your child's report card in school. Here is an example of a customer report card for a fast food restaurant and a hospital.

XYZ Restaurant Appreciates Your Comments:

	Excellent	Good	Fair	Poor	Very Bad
Cleanliness	☐	☐	☐	☐	☐
Food Quality	☐	☐	☐	☐	☐
Courtesy of Staff	☐	☐	☐	☐	☐
Prices	☐	☐	☐	☐	☐

ABC Hospital Appreciates Your Comments:

	Excellent	Good	Fair	Poor	Very Bad
Admission Procedure	☐	☐	☐	☐	☐
Quality of Care	☐	☐	☐	☐	☐
Professionalism of Staff	☐	☐	☐	☐	☐
Physicians	☐	☐	☐	☐	☐
Food	☐	☐	☐	☐	☐
Therapy Services	☐	☐	☐	☐	☐

You can see from these examples of comment or report cards that a company can quickly get a picture of how well they are servicing their customers. Analyzing the ratings can be done by assigning numbers to each verbal descriptor, such as Excellent being a 5 and Very Bad being a 1. You add up the scores to get an overall rating for the restaurant or the hospital. You can also average the scores within specific rating categories to determine which areas need the most attention.

Decide how you can adapt these comment or report card formats to your business.

Service Standards of Performance (SOP)

This has more to do with your employees than with your customers. Service SOPs are vitally important to your success in improving service quality and customer satisfaction. While it is true that service is intangible, and quite often a customer's level of satisfaction is highly subjective, there are employee behaviors that can be measured. It is these behaviors that you quantify as the service standards of performance.

Some examples include answering the telephone before the fourth ring, saying the customer's name at least once if you know it, always saying thank you to a customer, resolving complaints in a timely fashion and to the customer's satisfaction, responding to a customer within 30 seconds of their entering your store or facility, keeping time spent waiting in line under 5 minutes and completing a purchase or exchange transaction within a certain period of time. These are all possible objective standards of performance you can use. Complete the chart below to help you identify your service SOPs.

EMPLOYEE BEHAVIOR	SERVICE STANDARD
1.	
2.	
3.	
4.	
5.	

One thing you must remember about service SOPs. You are rating your employees on their abilities to service and satisfy your customers. When the employees receive high ratings from you or your customers, the employees should be rewarded and these behaviors reinforced. Service SOPs without an employee reward and recognition program will not help you improve your service quality and levels of customer satisfaction because employees will not feel their efforts are appreciated.

Customer Satisfaction Benchmarking

Benchmarking was mentioned earlier in this book as a method to measure and improve quality. To review, benchmarking is simply finding a company that is the best at something and comparing your efforts in the same area to theirs. You then adapt and modify their work to fit your situation to improve your service quality, and subsequently, your customer satisfaction.

Customer satisfaction benchmarking works the same way. Find a company, either in or out of your industry, that consistently receives high satisfaction ratings. Find out what it does in each area, how it does it, what and how it measures customer satisfaction, and then adapt its techniques to your company. Constant comparisons with the "best in class" will force you to improve your service quality and increase your levels of customer satisfaction.

Also, never forget about internal benchmarking. You should consistently measure the satisfaction levels of your customers and use each subsequent measurement as the benchmark for future measurements. This way, you have a basis for ongoing comparison within your own company.

SAMPLE INTERNAL BENCHMARK LOG FOR CUSTOMER SATISFACTION

Technique	12/1993	12/1994	12/1995	12/1996
Written Survey Focus Group Rating # Lost Customers % Lost Customers				

Attribute Ratings and Perceptual Maps

Many times, customers unknowingly compare one service attribute of your business with another, or they compare it with the same attribute from a competitor's business. Let's say you service computers, and you pride yourself in having a repair technician on-site in three hours or less. This speed of contact and repair is one of your service attributes. Customers can compare this with the quality of the repair your technician provides when he or she completes the job, or with the speed and availability of a competitor's repair person. In a restaurant, customers may compare how your food looks (the presentation attribute) with how it tastes.

You find out what attributes your customers are using to measure your service quality and their level of satisfaction by asking them, or reviewing your written and personal surveys to determine which key service areas keep coming up.

There are many ways to measure satisfaction based on service attributes. You can ask customers to rank order (prioritize) several key attributes in order of importance to them. Here is a sample.

Thank you for taking the time to complete this customer service form. Your answers will help us improve our service to you and increase your satisfaction with our services. Please rank order each item by placing a number from 1 to 10 next to the item, with 1 being the most important to you and 10 being the least important to you.

__ Courtesy   __ Speed with which we answer the phone

__ Knowledge of our staff   __ Availability of staff for assistance

__ Speed of complaint handling   __ Complaints handled to your satisfaction

__ Appearance of facility   __ Appearance of staff

__ Concern we show for customers   __ Level of service quality

---

This is just one format you can use to determine how your customers perceive the attributes of your service and how important these attributes are to them. Another format is to take one attribute and compare it against three or four others. Do this both within your company and against your competitors. When you do it against your competitors, you will learn how vulnerable you are to losing customers to them.

A sample comparison form:

In each pair of items below, please check the one that is most important to you when you visit us. Thank you.

____ Speed of service   ____ Speed of service

    or   or

____ Friendliness of personnel   ____ Number of services available

____ Speed of service   ____ Speed of service

    or   or

____ Knowledge of personnel   ____ Appearance of the office

ATTRIBUTE RATINGS AND PERCEPTUAL MAPS (continued)

The company would then count up the number of choices made for each option, and through these numbers alone, they could determine the desirability of "speed of service" when compared to the other service attributes. Of course, you may then want to ask your customers to rate each of the other attributes in comparison to each other, also.

When the counting is completed, the attributes can be placed on a scale in rank order, descending from the most important to the least important, to show how customers perceive the services you provide. Or they can be placed on a quadrant graph to depict their relationship. To do this, you use information from your surveys that tells you how well customers perceive you are performing on these service attributes. This way, you graph the importance of the attribute to the customer against your performance as perceived by the customer, giving you a pictorial representation of your customers' perception of your service to them in relation to what they perceive they need.

Importance of Service Attributes to Customers

1. Speed of service
2. Friendliness of personnel
3. Knowledge of personnel
4. Number of services available
5. Appearance of facility

The above table shows a possible priority order of attribute ranking assuming a sufficient number of customers have been polled. The graph below depicts the same service attributes on a perceptual map. This map shows the relationship of the importance of the service attribute to the customer with the customers' perception of how well the company is performing the service. Performance data comes from previous surveys or interviews, or you can modify the attribute rating scale to ask customers to rate your performance on the attribute along with its importance to them. An example is provided for you.

```
High

    1 speed                            2 friendliness




Importance              3 knowledge
                        _____


                                    4 services
                                  5 appearance




Low         Performance            High
```

Another thing you can do with a perceptual map is to ask your customers to compare you and several of your competitors on one or more key service attributes, both in importance and performance. Then, you can graph these results also. Graphing the results becomes extremely helpful when you are comparing your company to a competitor because you can determine your areas of strength, opportunity, weaknesses, and areas needing improvement.

In each pair of items below, please check the one that is most important to you when you visit us. Then, place a number from 1 to 5 next to each item to tell us how well you think we are performing on that item, with 5 indicating the best. Thank you.

___/___ Speed of service   ___/___ Speed of service

    or   or

___/___ Friendliness of personnel   ___/___ Number of services available

___/___ Speed of service   ___/___ Speed of service

    or   or

___/___ Knowledge of personnel   ___/___ Appearance of the facility

SUMMARY OF CUSTOMER SATISFACTION MEASUREMENT TECHNIQUES

You have now been introduced to a variety of customer satisfaction measurement techniques, ranging from written and telephone surveys to focus groups and personal interviews. You have also learned about reporting methods such as customer report cards, customer satisfaction index, benchmarking, attribute ratings and perceptual maps. There are many more sophisticated statistical tools and measurement techniques you can use, but they are beyond the scope of this book.

If you develop and implement some or all of these measurement and reporting techniques, you will have an excellent customer satisfaction measurement system to go along with your service quality measurement system.

An Important Reminder

You also want to collect demographic information on your customers (respondents). This information allows you to classify customers into categories and determine if people of the same neighborhood, income level or gender are responding similarly or differently to your surveys. The information you want to get includes name, address, zip code, age, gender, education level, type of job, personal and household income levels, number of family members, frequency of purchases or shopping visits, money spent on each purchase and number of people they can remember having referred. There are also other demographic characteristics you can collect information on, such as socioeconomic status, personal and professional organizations and community service activities. However, the basics of age, gender, zip, education and income are usually sufficient for a business to learn more about their customers. If you collect no other personal information on your customers, make certain you get these facts.

ANALYZING RESULTS AND FOLLOWING UP

Once you have measured your customer satisfaction levels, you must analyze the results so that you can either implement improvements suggested in the surveys or follow-up directly with customers to have them expand on their comments. Your analysis and follow-up will also provide your staff with indications as to the effectiveness of their performance and benchmarks against which to gauge future service performances.

Statistical Procedures

Most companies use very simple statistical procedures to analyze their quality and customer satisfaction data. More sophisticated statistical techniques than the ones described here can be found in a statistics textbook.

There are at least five measures you should be aware of as you analyze your data:

1. **Mean**	The average of all the scores or responses to a question, and to a complete survey.
2. **Median**	The score that is in the exact middle of all the responses.
3. **Mode**	The score that appears the most in the responses of customers.
4. **Standard Deviation**	How much a score can deviate or vary from the mean (average). You use the standard deviation when you calculate the upper and lower limits of your control charts when measuring quality.
5. **Range**	The difference between the highest and lowest score on a question.

You can also use the frequency distribution that you developed from your check sheet when measuring quality. Just follow the exact same procedures for creating frequency intervals. The same holds true for the histogram, which will give you a graphic representation of the distribution of your data.

ANALYZING RESULTS AND FOLLOWING UP (continued)

Ratios and Percentages

Many companies find it easier to use ratios and percentages to classify and analyze their data. Again, some of the data may be collected as words (excellent, good, fair, poor) and then be converted to numbers. While statisticians may cringe, this has become accepted practice when measuring your customer satisfaction levels. The goal is to achieve a rating or percentage score so you can relate performance to it.

This percentage also serves as a benchmark for future efforts. Notice in the appendix following the Omni Hotel survey how their report identifies percentages within each response category and an overall year to date category.

Percentages are simple to calculate and use. Just total up the scores and divide that by the maximum total score possible on a question or in a category. That will give you a percentage rating. For example, if a question is answered by 10 people, and the highest score on the question can be a 5 (Exceeds Expectations or Extremely Satisfied), the highest possible total would be a 50. Now, if these 10 people all responded to that question with a 4 (Slightly Above Expectations or Very Satisfied), the total of the responses would be 40. 40/50=80%, so your percentage score on this question would be 80%. You can use this score to compare it with other questions and categories on the survey, against last year's results, and as a benchmark for future results.

Depending on your requirements, you may need to get into more sophisticated statistical analyses. I recommend you check with a statistician or statistics textbook. Remember though, it is vitally important to the success of your quality improvement program and your provision of service leading to customer satisfaction that you and your staff understand the results of your statistical analysis.

What gets measured gets done, and what gets analyzed gets followed up on. Keep your measurement system and your analysis programs simple so everyone can understand them and work with them.

P A R T

IV

Managing Customer Satisfaction

MANAGING SERVICE QUALITY AND CUSTOMER SATISFACTION

Now that you know how to measure quality and customer satisfaction, you must know what to do with your information. Companies have two choices. They can be **proactive,** and begin the service and satisfaction management process before they even come in contact with customers, or they can be **reactive,** and wait for customers to complain or tell them what to do. Some companies behave in both ways. However, I recommend you do as much as possible to proactively manage your quality and customer satisfaction efforts.

What are you doing now to manage these activities?

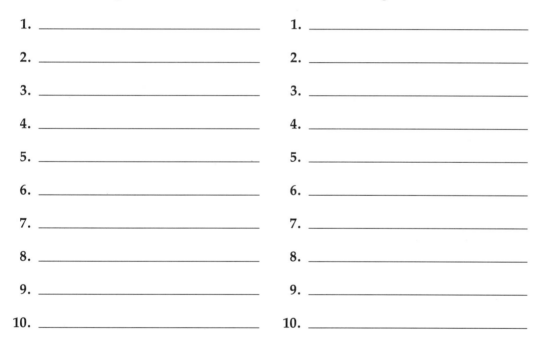

Proactive Management Efforts

1. _____
2. _____
3. _____
4. _____
5. _____
6. _____
7. _____
8. _____
9. _____
10. _____

Reactive Management Efforts

1. _____
2. _____
3. _____
4. _____
5. _____
6. _____
7. _____
8. _____
9. _____
10. _____

Although there are 10 lines under each column heading in the table, you are not obligated to only completing the ten, nor are you obligated to complete the entire list if you are not doing that many things. Hopefully, your proactive column will be longer than your reactive column.

PROACTIVE MANAGEMENT

Here are 10 things you can do to proactively manage your service quality and customer satisfaction. Doing some of them will ensure you a larger customer base; doing all of them will possibly make you the market leader in your field. One thing is for sure: when you implement these 10 suggestions into your business, your levels of quality and customer satisfaction will definitely increase.

1. **Everyone Works For the Customer** — You must become a customer-focused organization, totally and completely. You and your employees do not work for the company; you work for the customer. Without customers, there is no business and no company. Therefore, you must place customers on the highest pedestal possible and do everything you can to ensure their satisfaction.

2. **Get To Know Your Customers Intimately** — Companies that know their customers intimately are much more profitable than their competitors. This is because these companies are giving customers exactly what they want and ask for. Talk to your customers directly. Write them. Call them up. Ask them questions. Survey them. Invite them to your facility. Take them to lunch or dinner. Court them. Do anything and everything you can to learn about who they are; what they need, want and expect; and how they want you to give it to them. Then, give it to them just that way, even if it means modifying your current product or service or policies.

3. **Build Quality In** — Once you know what your customers want from you, you can give it to them at the highest level of quality possible. Remember that quality is whatever the customer says it is, and it can change daily. You must build quality into your products and services from the start. Quality is like a wellness program for your business. You use good preventive medical techniques to ensure the "healthiest" (i.e., highest quality) product or service possible.

4. **Develop a Passionate Customer Focus** — Being customer focused is no longer enough. That will make you barely competitive as every company believes they are customer focused. You must be **passionate** about your customers. LOVE them as you would have them love you. Your customer focus must be so deep and dedicated that it permeates your personal being and the life of your business. Customers are the lifeblood of your business, so treat them with care, affection and attention.

5. **Train The Staff** — This is one of the most critical elements in producing quality and achieving customer satisfaction. Customer service and quality improvement is everyone's job, so you must train your staff in the technical aspects of their work as well as the service-related aspects of it. Everyone gives service to the customers, not just the "customer service department." In fact, you may want to think about not having a customer service department. This forces everyone to rely only on themselves to take the responsibility of serving and satisfying the customer.

6. **Empower The Staff** — Training the staff to build in quality, to provide superior customer service and to take the responsibility for satisfying the customers is still not enough. You must also empower the staff with the authority to do **whatever it takes to guarantee the customer is satisfied.** No passing the buck to another employee or having to get a manager's approval on a refund or an exchange. Everyone should have the authority to do **whatever it takes,** whenever the customer wants it, to ensure total customer satisfaction. When you empower your staff you will find their commitment to their jobs, the business and the customers greatly increases.

7. **Measure, Measure, Measure** — Measure everything. There are two important reasons for this: 1) What gets measured gets done; and 2) You must measure it to improve it. Therefore, measure the performance of yourself and your staff. Measure the quality of the products and services you produce and sell. Measure the satisfaction levels and service perceptions of your customers. Then, make the appropriate and necessary positive changes based on the results of these measurements.

8. **Recognize and Reward** — Recognize and reward both your employees and your customers. Show your employees appreciation for a job well done. Let them know you care about them as people, not just as workers. Show your customers you appreciate their business. Let them know you care about them as people also, not just buyers of your product or service. When you recognize people for their efforts, the rewards should be meaningful, and this does not mean they necessarily have to be monetary. People crave recognition for their efforts. I used to give out stickers that had JWD printed on them, for a "Job Well Done." I also give out smiley faces. Both things show people I care and appreciate their efforts. For customers, I send them thank-you cards, holiday cards and gifts. What do you do to recognize and reward your employees and customers?

PROACTIVE MANAGEMENT (continued)

9. **Go Out Of Your Way** — Everyone is looking for and expecting value for their money. All your competitors are trumpeting their quality and value. You must differentiate your business by going out of your way for customers. Give them as many value added benefits as possible. Do everything you can think of to satisfy the customer that the customer did not or would not expect from you. In fact, take your passionate customer focus and develop it to the point that customer satisfaction is not enough. Now, you must "wow" and "delight" your customers. What can you do, how can you go out of your way to create what I call the "WOW Factor"? This is when customers who do business with you are so delighted that they come away saying "WOW."

10. **Make It Better** — Some businesses survey their customers and find out the customers believe they are getting quality products and services and they are very satisfied. Then, the businesses get complacent and begin to rest on their laurels. You cannot do that in today's economy and competitive environment. If your customers tell you that your quality is excellent and your service is superb and they are highly satisfied with the way you treat them, you must immediately look for ways to make everything you are doing better.

Quality can always be improved, just as customer satisfaction levels can be increased. These increments may be ever so slight, but that is why we call them continuous, incremental improvements. Don't be one of those companies that believes "If it ain't broke, don't fix it." Be one of the new breed of passionate, customer-focused companies that believes "If it ain't broke, make it better." If you don't, your competitors will and your customers will then go to them.

MEASURING SERVICE PERFORMANCE

Service-quality improvement and customer-satisfaction surveys determine how the customer thinks you are doing. Internally, you must measure the service performance of your employees. I mentioned earlier in the book how important this was, and it is so important, it bears repeating.

You must develop objective standards to measure service performance. Things like answering the telephone by the fourth ring, keeping a caller on hold for no more than 30 seconds before getting back to him or her, returning telephone calls within 24 hours, responding to written correspondence within 24 hours, sending a technician to a site within 3 hours, shipping orders within 24 hours, sending replacement parts within 12 hours, or same-day service. You get the idea.

Remember that if you do not or cannot measure it, you cannot improve it. If you are having difficulty developing measurements for your service performances (and this happens often because services are intangible), ask your employees for help. Not only will they come up with objective measurement standards, they will be more likely to accept and buy-in to those standards since they had a role in developing them.

Use this simple chart to help you start to develop your service standards of performance.

GOAL	BEHAVIOR	STANDARD

You now have several ways to measure your service quality and customer satisfaction. Plus, you have some ideas on how to effectively and successfully manage your customer service system. The last section of the book covers a very important topic, and that is the development of strategic partnerships or alliances with your customers. But first, a brief commentary about managing customer complaints.

MANAGING CUSTOMER COMPLAINTS

One of the most influential factors related to customer satisfaction and perception of service quality is how you handle customer complaints. Unfortunately, many customers judge a company by how well they respond to complaints, refund requests or exchanges. In a nutshell, accept all refund requests and exchanges graciously, make them quickly, and do not question the customers as to why they are requesting the refund or making the exchange. Unconditional service will take you much further than anything else in developing satisfied customers who remain loyal and refer other customers.

When a customer comes to you with a complaint, don't view it as a problem. View it as a golden opportunity. Your customers, who have taken their valuable time to contact you with this complaint, are also going to provide you with FREE information about how you can improve your business. They will also be telling you exactly what to do to make certain you satisfy them now and in the future. Listen to their complaint. Question them for more information. Beg them if you have to. Just make sure you find out exactly what the customer wants and then give it to him or her.

In my previous book, *Beyond Customer Service,* I told you that up to 75% of your customers who complain will do business with you again. I also told you that the key to managing customer complaints was a well-trained staff and an active recovery and restitution process. Recovery and restitution related to customer complaints and subsequent satisfaction is so important to your success, and future sales, that I will repeat the five-step process here. For a more detailed description, see page 41 in *Beyond Customer Service.*

Service Recovery Program: Managing Complaints

1. **Apologize** — Let your customer know you are sorry for the inconvenience. Even if it was not your fault, and regardless of who is at fault, apologize first to the customer. Tell them you are going to take full responsibility to resolve the complaint.

2. **Urgent Reinstatement (Restatement)** — Restate the complaint in your own words to make sure you understand the exact nature of the complaint and you and the customer are in complete agreement. Tell the customer again, and show him or her, if possible, that you are going to do everything possible to resolve the problem.

3. **Empathy** — Communicate clearly to the customer that you understand the problem and appreciate the way he or she feels. Also, emphasize that you are glad he or she brought this to your attention because it gives you an opportunity to correct the situation.

4. **Restitution** — Do whatever it takes at this point to satisfy the customer. Give the customer whatever he or she needs or wants or expects from you to resolve the complaint without giving away the store. After you resolve the complaint, go the extra mile and give the customer something else: a discount coupon, a free gift, or allow him or her to purchase another item at a sale price. Do something extra to add value to what might have been a bad situation.

5. **Follow Up** — Check with all customers before they leave to make sure they are satisfied. Then, call them and write them a note within a week of the complaint resolution to make certain they are still satisfied. You may even want to include a sales coupon with your note. Make sure you continue to keep in touch with the customer.

Turning Complaints into Sales

There is no better time to try to upsell or make a new sale to customers than when you have resolved a complaint to their satisfaction. If you have listened carefully, focused on one complaint at a time and resolved it, and made a value-added offer to the customer just to show your appreciation for giving you the opportunity to resolve the complaint, then you are ready to make another sale.

Think about it. Your customer is now extremely satisfied with what you have done. He or she is in a great mood and very happy to do business with you. All you have to do is build on this momentum to create an additional sale.

STRATEGIC CUSTOMER PARTNERSHIPS

Success in business today is dependent upon providing a quality product or service enhanced by superior customer service, leading to total customer satisfaction and hopefully, repeat purchases and referrals from satisfied customers. One way to increase your chances of achieving all these things is to create strategic partnerships or alliances with your customers.

You do this by inviting your customers into your business. I am not talking about financially; rather, I am talking about literally inviting them in to see how you conduct your business. Take them on a tour of your facility or plant. Show them your offices. If you work at home, meet with them and tell them how you run your business, what type of equipment you have, and how you have set everything up to serve them better.

Ask them what you can do to help them achieve something. They are in business too, or they must have something they want to achieve. Ask them how you can help them achieve it. What can you do for them to save them time, money, make them healthier, happier, or capable of doing their job better. Become their customer in some way, even if there is no exchange of money.

Now, you both have a stake in each other's success. That is what strategic partnering is all about. Each partner does whatever it takes to help the other partner be more successful. Here are some questions you can ask to decide which customers should become your strategic partners.

1. **With whom do I do the majority of my business?** (List all the companies or people.)

   _____

   _____

   _____

   _____

   _____

   _____

2. What is it they need, want or expect from me?

_____

_____

_____

_____

3. Have I determined their perception of my service quality?

_____ Yes   _____ No

4. Have I determined their level of customer satisfaction?

_____ Yes   _____ No

5. Do I have to develop these programs first before attempting to create a strategic partnership?

_____ Yes   _____ No

6. If Yes to #3 & 4: What do I know that my customers need that I can give them?

_____

_____

_____

_____

7. How can we both benefit by working more closely together?

_____

_____

_____

_____

STRATEGIC CUSTOMER PARTNERSHIPS
(continued)

8. **What are the obstacles, problems or objections that I can foresee when I approach my customer about forming a strategic partnership?** (Consider time, money, effort, etc.)

    _____

    _____

    _____

    _____

    _____

9. **What types of networked alliances can I help my customers form?**

    _____

    _____

    _____

    _____

    _____

10. **How will this or these strategic partnerships benefit my other customers?**

    _____

    _____

    _____

    _____

There you have it. Ten questions to help you form strategic partnerships with your customers. The end result will be superior quality in your products and services for them, improved levels of customer service that you will provide to them, and increased levels of customer satisfaction. These will result in repeat purchases, more referrals, and increased business and profitability for you.

Focus passionately on your customers. Do whatever it takes to learn about their needs, wants, expectations and desires. Give them whatever you can that is within your power. Give your employees the training and the authority to do the same.

Measure everything you do within your business, and measure everything you do related to your customers. Get your customers to define quality for you, then measure it. Get them to define superior customer service, give it to them and then measure it accordingly. Get them to tell you how to satisfy them do it, and then measure it. And, once you have collected all these measurements through some or all of the techniques described in this book, analyze your measurements and find out where you can improve. By measuring quality and customer satisfaction, you will become more customer focused, and that will help you be successful.

P A R T

V

Appendix: Customer Service/Satisfaction Surveys

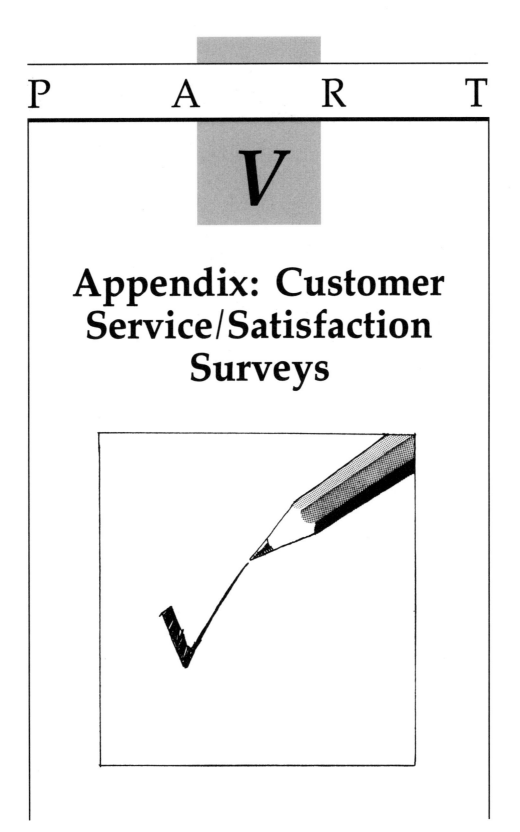

SAMPLE SURVEY

Here is a sample survey provided by a bank. The original survey only had four scaled responses to it and also asked customers to rate as many service providers as possible on one survey card. I have made certain changes to align the survey with the principles of this book and to make it easier for you to adapt the questions and approach to your own business.

BANK CUSTOMER SATISFACTION SURVEY

Please give us your comments . . .

Date of Visit _____   Time of Visit _____   Branch Visited _____

These comments pertain to (please check one service provider):

_____ Inside Teller   _____ Drive-in Teller   _____ Branch Manager

_____ Consumer Lender   _____ Customer Service Representative

_____ Mortgage Lender   _____ General Comments

1. Please tell us how satisfied you were with the following:

	Very Satisfied	Satisfied	Somewhat Satisfied	Dissatisfied	Very Dissatisfied
a. Courtesy/Personal attention	5	4	3	2	1
b. Time spent waiting for service	5	4	3	2	1
c. Knowledge level of employees	5	4	3	2	1
d. Number of services provided	5	4	3	2	1
e. Accuracy	5	4	3	2	1
f. Appearance of branch	5	4	3	2	1

2. If you received particularly good service, or particularly poor service, we would like to know. Please write your comments below.

_____

_____

_____

3. What suggestions can you make for us to improve our service to you?

_____

_____

_____

4. Would you like us to contact you? If so, please fill in the information below.

Name: _____   Telephone: _____   Best Time to Call:_____

Thank you for your time and assistance.

RESTAURANT SURVEYS

Here are two samples of standard customer comment cards you will find at many restaurants. Notice first that both only use a four-point scale, so if you want to adapt them, I recommend you add a fifth point. Also, notice how these cards invite diners to fill them out by offering a chance for a free dinner on one card and the possibility of winning $100.00 on the other. You can be sure that if your restaurant (or business) will go to the expense of giving away free meals or money just to get customers to fill out comment cards, then you are definitely customer focused and customer committed. Finally, both cards tell the customer they can mail it in and the postage is prepaid. If you want customers to mail their comments, you pay for the postage.

YOUR COMMENTS COULD BE WORTH CASH

We value your comments as a customer to determine if we are meeting your expectations. To show our appreciation for your sincere comments, we will be entering this card into a drawing in which you could win. Simply drop this card at the cash register as you leave or drop it in the mail (no postage necessary) and you will be automatically entered into the drawing. Drawings will be held on a monthly basis. (1st day of every month.)

Date: _____ Time: _____ a.m./p.m.
Location: _____

	Excellent	Good	Fair	Poor
Courteous & Helpful Employees	[ ]	[ ]	[ ]	[ ]
Fast & Accurate Service	[ ]	[ ]	[ ]	[ ]
Product Quality	[ ]	[ ]	[ ]	[ ]
Cleanliness of Restaurant	[ ]	[ ]	[ ]	[ ]
Value	[ ]	[ ]	[ ]	[ ]

Items Purchased: _____

How often do you visit this restaurant?
Once a Week or More [ ]   Every 2-3 Weeks [ ]   Once a Month [ ]   Less Often [ ]   First Time [ ]

Party Size: 1 Person [ ]   2-3 [ ]   4-5 [ ]   Over 5 [ ]

Based on today's experience, would you return? Yes [ ]   No [ ]

Ideas/Comments: _____
_____

Name: _____
Address: _____
City: _____ State: _____ Zip: _____
Phone: _____

Lunch ☐   Supper ☐   Date _____

Location:

We Value Your Opinion — We would appreciate a moment of your time in completing this card. Your satisfaction is important to us. Please fill in this card and drop in comment box at register or mail it in. **Thank You.**

How do you rate Our . . .	Excellent	Good	Fair	Poor
Food — Quality				
Portions				
Value (Price)				
Service — Quality				
Speed of Service				
Courtesy				
Cleanliness — Dining Room				
Restrooms				
Take-Out — Food				
Service				

How did you hear about us? _____

What did you like best about us? _____
_____

What would you change if you could? _____
_____

What menu items would you like to see added? _____
_____

What did you have to eat today? _____
_____

Any Comments/Suggestions or Ideas? _____
_____
_____

— OPTIONAL —

Name _____   Phone _____

Address _____
_____

*Please drop this card in the suggestion box located in the register area. This makes you eligible for our Weekly Drawing.

HOSPITAL EMPLOYEE OPINION SURVEY

This employee opinion survey was developed by me on Survey Pro software for a hospital client. An internal employee opinion or attitude survey is the same as a customer service/satisfaction survey. Use and modify the statements and identified areas to determine the satisfaction levels of your internal customers, your employees. You may want to change the scale from "Agreement" to "Satisfaction."

GENERAL HOSPITAL EMPLOYEE OPINION SURVEY

INSTRUCTIONS: Place a mark in the box that most closely corresponds to your level of agreement with the question or statement. Do not put your name or department on the form. Thank you for your participation.

	Strongly Agree	Agree	Neutral	Disagree	Strongly Disagree
1. I like my job	☐	☐	☐	☐	☐
2. The amount of work I do seems to be more important than the quality of the work I do	☐	☐	☐	☐	☐
3. My job performance is evaluated in a timely manner	☐	☐	☐	☐	☐
4. Employees are frequently recognized for a job well done	☐	☐	☐	☐	☐
5. The equipment I work with is in good and safe operating condition	☐	☐	☐	☐	☐
6. The people I work with are cooperative and pleasant	☐	☐	☐	☐	☐
7. I am happy with the hospital's sick leave policy	☐	☐	☐	☐	☐
8. I received an appropriate amount of training and orientation for my job	☐	☐	☐	☐	☐
9. It is easy to obtain equipment and supplies	☐	☐	☐	☐	☐
10. I feel pressured in my job	☐	☐	☐	☐	☐
11. The employees in my department work as a team	☐	☐	☐	☐	☐

	Strongly Agree	Agree	Neutral	Disagree	Strongly Disagree
12. Administration does a good job of keeping the employees informed about the hospital	☐	☐	☐	☐	☐
13. The future of the hospital looks secure	☐	☐	☐	☐	☐
14. My supervisor values my input and opinions	☐	☐	☐	☐	☐
15. I respect administrative decisions	☐	☐	☐	☐	☐
16. I would recommend the hospital to my family	☐	☐	☐	☐	☐
17. There is a caring attitude toward patients by the staff in the hospital	☐	☐	☐	☐	☐
18. There is a caring attitude toward the staff by other staff members	☐	☐	☐	☐	☐
19. My supervisor helps me solve problems as they arise	☐	☐	☐	☐	☐
20. It is safe to say what you think about hospital operations	☐	☐	☐	☐	☐
21. Salaries and benefits are comparable with other hospitals of this size	☐	☐	☐	☐	☐
22. Work is distributed equally within my department	☐	☐	☐	☐	☐
23. I am happy with the hospital's vacation policy	☐	☐	☐	☐	☐
24. I am almost always able to take my break and lunch period	☐	☐	☐	☐	☐
25. The hospital is well maintained	☐	☐	☐	☐	☐
26. My supervisor makes decisions that I perceive as fair	☐	☐	☐	☐	☐
27. My job is secure as long as I do good work	☐	☐	☐	☐	☐

HOSPITAL EMPLOYEE OPINION SURVEY
(continued)

	Strongly Agree	Agree	Neutral	Disagree	Strongly Disagree
28. The hospital has a good reputation in the community	☐	☐	☐	☐	☐
29. My performance evaluations are helpful	☐	☐	☐	☐	☐
30. My supervisor does a good job of building teamwork	☐	☐	☐	☐	☐
31. I would be a patient at this hospital	☐	☐	☐	☐	☐
32. I would recommend this hospital to friends and neighbors	☐	☐	☐	☐	☐
33. The hospital's health insurance package is satisfactory	☐	☐	☐	☐	☐
34. Administration is open to new ideas and methods	☐	☐	☐	☐	☐
35. The patient (customer) pays my salary	☐	☐	☐	☐	☐

36. The three things I like most about working here are: _____

_____

_____

_____

37. The three things I like least about working here are: _____

_____

_____

_____

38. Each week, I work the following number of hours (fill in blank). _____

39. If I could change one thing about the hospital, it would be: _____

_____

_____

_____

40. This survey will help make the hospital a better place to work.

☐ Strongly Agree ☐ Agree ☐ Neutral ☐ Disagree ☐ Strongly Disagree

BUSINESS OFFICE CUSTOMER SATISFACTION SURVEY

This brief customer satisfaction survey was developed by me for the business office of a hospital client. Pay attention to the items being questioned in the survey. These items were defined by the business office, rather than by the customers themselves, as being important to the customer. If you have designed your survey in this manner, make sure you analyze the responses carefully. If you are getting several or many low number ratings, perhaps you are not measuring what the customer defines as satisfaction with your product or service.

CUSTOMER SATISFACTION SURVEY

We would appreciate your help in telling us how we can improve the services of our hospital and our business office. Please respond to the following 15 statements by using the 5-point scale below. Thank you for your assistance in helping us improve.

1	2	3	4	5
Much Less Than Expected	Less Than Expected	As Expected	More Than Expected	Much More Than Expected

Admitting

1. The smoothness of the admitting process was . . . _____
2. The courtesy and politeness of the admitting staff was . . . _____
3. The speed of the admissions process was . . . _____
4. The concern showed towards me by the admitting staff was . . . _____
5. The ease with which I found the admitting office within the hospital was . . . _____

Business Office

6. The ease with which I was able to read my billing statement was . . . _____
7. The ease with which I was able to understand my billing statement was . . . _____
8. The courtesy of the staff at the business office was . . . _____
9. The cooperation I received from the staff at the business office was . . . _____

BUSINESS OFFICE CUSTOMER SATISFACTION SURVEY (continued)

10. The speed with which my questions were answered was . . .   _____
11. The manner in which the business office handled my complaint was . . .   _____
12. The ease with which I found the business office was . . .   _____
13. The promptness of the business office in answering the telephone was . . .   _____
14. The treatment I received from the business office staff was . . .   _____
15. The assistance I received from the business office staff was . . .   _____

If you have any other comments you would like to make, or if there is anything else you would like us to know about, please write in the space below. Also, please give us the name of the employee who provided you with exceptional service or poor service, if this was the case. Your comments will be kept in the strictest confidence.

NAME: (optional) _____

ADDRESS: _____

CITY: _____ STATE: _____ ZIP: _____

TELEPHONE: _____

THANK YOU FOR HELPING US IMPROVE OUR SERVICE TO YOU.

HOTEL CUSTOMER SATISFACTION SURVEY

This sample survey is currently being used by Omni Hotels. It is quite extensive and inclusive, covering as many areas of the hotel and hospitality experience as possible. Notice how the survey uses a five-point scale for ease of scoring. Also, following the survey, I have reprinted one of the reports Omni Hotels gives to its general managers. This follow-up report is critical to their customer-satisfaction efforts. It gives the general managers and the staff information on how their hotel did within a specified period of time, and also compares current satisfaction ratings within categories and overall to other benchmarks, such as last year.

You may want to adapt the response scale, as I have already suggested to Omni Hotels, to include answers ranging from Very Satisfied to Very Dissatisfied or Exceeds Expectations to Does Not Meet Expectations. You should be aware that Omni Hotels is in the process of revising and improving this evaluation survey based on customer feedback.

OMNI ✤ INNER HARBOR HOTEL

101 West Fayette Street, Baltimore, Maryland 21201

GUEST EVALUATION

Room Number: _____

	Excellent	Good	Average	Fair	Poor
1. On an overall basis, how did our hotel meet your expectations?	☐	☐	☐	☐	☐
2. Overall, how welcome did our staff make you feel?	☐	☐	☐	☐	☐
3. Overall, how would you rate the hotel's value for the price paid?	☐	☐	☐	☐	☐

4. Was your room reservation in order upon your arrival?   ☐ Yes   ☐ No

5. Please give your assessment of the hospitality and efficiency in the following hotel services: *(Please check appropriate box)*

	Excellent	Good	Average	Fair	Poor
A. Reservations					
Hospitality	☐	☐	☐	☐	☐
Efficiency	☐	☐	☐	☐	☐
B. Doorman/Bell Services					
Hospitality	☐	☐	☐	☐	☐
Efficiency	☐	☐	☐	☐	☐
C. Check-In Process					
Hospitality	☐	☐	☐	☐	☐
Efficiency	☐	☐	☐	☐	☐
D. Cleanliness and Housekeeping					
Hospitality	☐	☐	☐	☐	☐
Efficiency	☐	☐	☐	☐	☐
E. Telephone Message Service					
Hospitality	☐	☐	☐	☐	☐
Efficiency	☐	☐	☐	☐	☐
F. Parking					
Hospitality	☐	☐	☐	☐	☐
Efficiency	☐	☐	☐	☐	☐
G. Check-Out					
Hospitality	☐	☐	☐	☐	☐
Efficiency	☐	☐	☐	☐	☐
H. Room Comfort	☐	☐	☐	☐	☐

6. Was everything in working order?   ☐ Yes   ☐ No
If No, please tell us what was not in working order.

_____

_____

_____

7. If you reported the problem, was it corrected promptly?   ☐ Yes   ☐ No

8. Restaurant *(please specify name)*: _____

Meal Period: _____ Breakfast   _____ Lunch   _____ Dinner

Please rate the quality of the following:	Excellent	Good	Average	Fair	Poor
A. Meal Service	☐	☐	☐	☐	☐
B. Quality of Food	☐	☐	☐	☐	☐
C. Value for Price Paid	☐	☐	☐	☐	☐

9. Room Service

	Excellent	Good	Average	Fair	Poor
A. Prompt Delivery/Service	☐	☐	☐	☐	☐
B. Quality of Food	☐	☐	☐	☐	☐

10. Banquet/Meeting Events

	Excellent	Good	Average	Fair	Poor
A. Service	☐	☐	☐	☐	☐
B. Quality of Food	☐	☐	☐	☐	☐
C. Facilities	☐	☐	☐	☐	☐

11. If you are enrolled in the Omni Select Guest Program, how would you rate your Select Guest services and benefits during this visit?   ☐ ☐ ☐ ☐ ☐

12. If your travels should bring you to this area, would you stay with us again?   ☐ Yes   ☐ No

13. Would you stay at other Omni Hotels in the future as a result of your experience at this Omni Hotel?   ☐ Yes   ☐ No

14. Which members of our staff were especially helpful? Please let us know who they are and how they were helpful so that we can show them our appreciation.

Name _____

Position/Comments _____

_____

_____

Other Comments: _____

_____

_____

_____

_____

_____

_____

_____

PLEASE PROVIDE THE FOLLOWING INFORMATION *(Optional)*:

Please print:
Departure Date: ____/____/____ Length of Stay: _____

Name _____

Preferred Mailing Address _____

City _____ State _____ Zip _____

Telephone (____) _____

This information is strictly confidential and for evaluation response purposes only.

OMNI GUEST EVALUATION -

EVALUATION REPORT (SD663)

FOR THE PERIOD 12/01/91 THROUGH 12/31/91

PAGE   17
DATE 01/06/92
TIME 10:25 PM

	# RESPONSES		% EXCEED (1/2)		% BELOW (4/5)		% EXCEL (1)		% POOR (5)		EVALUATION INDEX		
	PER	YTD	PER	YTD	PER	YTD	PER	YTD	PER	YTD	PER	YTD	LYTD
OVERALL BASIS, MEET EXPECTATIONS	731	7997	90	97	1	1	79	76	--	1	93.9	92.7	86.9
OVERALL, DID WE MAKE YOU WELCOME	620	6162	97	96	1	1	77	77	--	--	93.2	92.0	88.2
VALUE FOR PRICE PAID	509	5701	94	91	2	3	68	65	--	1	89.9	87.9	80.9

	NUMBER OF RESPONSES			PERCENT YES			PERCENT NO			DID NOT RESPOND		
	PER	YTD	LYTD	PER	YTD	LYTD	PER	YTD	LYTD	PER	YTD	LYTD
WAS ROOM RESERVATION IN ORDER	456	4673	3556	90	97	94	2	3	6	289	3519	2305

	# RESPONSES		% EXCEED (1/2)		% BELOW (4/5)		% EXCEL (1)		% POOR (5)		EVALUATION INDEX		
	PER	YTD	PER	YTD	PER	YTD	PER	YTD	PER	YTD	PER	YTD	LYTD
HOSPITALITY OF STAFF													
RESERVATIONS	535	4864	98	96	1	1	76	75			93.3	92.5	87.1
DOORMAN/BELL SERVICES	527	4837	97	95	1	1	77	76		1	93.0	92.4	87.6
FRONT DESK RECEPTIONIST	535	4924	97	95	1	2	76	74			93.2	91.6	85.5
HOUSEKEEPING	542	4955	97	95	1	2	76	74			93.0	91.6	86.6
TELEPHONE OPERATORS	474	4034	95	95	1	1	74	74		1	91.8	91.7	83.4
PARKING	438	3622	94	93	3	2	75	70			91.6	89.9	84.3
FRONT DESK CASHIER	460	3664	90	95		1	78	74			93.7	91.8	87.5
EFFICIENCY OF STAFF													
RESERVATIONS	524	4677	90	95	1	2	75	73			92.9	91.5	84.7
DOORMAN/BELL SERVICES	517	4640	97	95	2	1	76	75		1	92.5	92.0	86.6
CHECK-IN PROCESS	521	4750	97	94	1	2	75	73			97.0	91.3	83.3
CLEANLINESS AND HOUSEKEEPING	529	4823	96	93	2	2	75	72		1	92.5	90.5	84.2
TELEPHONE MESSAGE SERVICE	463	3909	93	94	2	2	73	74		2	90.7	91.2	81.5
PARKING	429	3494	93	91	3	3	74	68			91.0	88.8	81.9
CHECKOUT, SPEED AND EFFICIENCY	461	3565	97	95	1		77	73		1	93.2	91.6	85.1
COMFORT OF ROOM	510	4631	97	95		1	77	75		1	93.4	91.9	86.6

	NUMBER OF RESPONSES			PERCENT YES			PERCENT NO			DID NOT RESPOND		
	PER	YTD	LYTD	PER	YTD	LYTD	PER	YTD	LYTD	PER	YTD	LYTD
WAS EVERYTHING IN WORKING ORDER	493	4590	3012	88	91	83	12	9	17	252	3602	2849
WAS PROBLEM CORRECTED PROMPTLY	96	1208	706	86	92	76	14	8	24	649	6904	5075

OTHER SAMPLE INVENTORIES

Here are several customer service and customer-satisfaction inventories reprinted from another Crisp book, *Beyond Customer Service*. They are included here to give you more ideas on the types of things you can measure. Also, you can always include questions or statements related to the quality of your products and services, and how satisfied customers are with that quality.

SERVICE RATING SCALE

Using a scale of 1 to 10 with 10 being the best, please rate how well you and your staff provide each of the following services:

Service	Self	Staff
a. Prompt and courteous answering of the telephones	_____	_____
b. Accurate responses to telephone inquiries	_____	_____
c. Providing individualized and personalized attention to each client	_____	_____
d. Marketing and promoting the business to current and new clients	_____	_____
e. Marketing and promoting the business to professional and other referral sources	_____	_____
f. Communicating prices and billing procedures clearly and concisely	_____	_____
g. Providing high quality, courteous and friendly service to all clients	_____	_____
h. Requesting and quickly resolving customer complaints	_____	_____
i. Keeping clients informed and updated about current and new developments regarding the business	_____	_____
j. Tracking the effectiveness of marketing and service efforts	_____	_____

CUSTOMER SERVICE INVENTORY

We are interested in finding out what you think about our services. Please respond to each statement by placing the number of the appropriate response in the blank space next to the statement.

1	2	3	4	5
Never	*Once in a while*	*Half the time*	*Often*	*Very Often*

_____ **1.** The telephone is answered by the third ring.

_____ **2.** The person answering the telephone is courteous and friendly.

_____ **3.** I am placed on hold for more than 30 seconds.

_____ **4.** My call is directed to the appropriate person.

_____ **5.** The office (store) is conveniently located and easy to find.

_____ **6.** There is ample parking available near the office (store).

_____ **7.** The atmosphere of the office (store) is warm and inviting.

_____ **8.** The regularly scheduled office (store) hours are convenient for me.

_____ **9.** The salesperson or the service provider greets me immediately.

_____ **10.** I wait less than 15 minutes if my appointment is delayed.

_____ **11.** Prices are appropriate for the products and services provided.

_____ **12.** Payment terms for the products or services are flexible.

_____ **13.** Payment methods are acceptable.

_____ **14.** I receive good value for my money.

_____ **15.** The office (store) staff is courteous and friendly.

CUSTOMER SERVICE INVENTORY
(continued)

_____ **16.** The service provider and/or staff is courteous and friendly.

_____ **17.** I receive personalized attention and service.

_____ **18.** My complaints are resolved quickly and to my satisfaction.

_____ **19.** The service provider and/or staff answers all my questions to my satisfaction.

_____ **20.** The service provider and/or staff is concerned about my situation.

_____ **21.** I am involved in decisions regarding my purchase.

_____ **22.** I feel comfortable with the personality of the service provider (staff).

_____ **23.** I am kept informed of all details regarding my purchase.

_____ **24.** I am happy with the way the service provider (staff) treats me.

_____ **25.** I feel the service provider (staff) is qualified to provide me with these services.

_____ **26.** I prefer to use these services rather than those provided by someone else.

_____ **27.** I can schedule an appointment or shop at the store when it is convenient for me.

_____ **28.** I will use this service provider (store) again.

_____ **29.** I would refer people to this service provider (store).

_____ **30.** The overall quality of the service is high.

Thank you for completing this inventory. Your answers will help us to understand your needs and improve the quality of the services we offer to you.

CUSTOMER SATISFACTION SURVEY

We are interested in finding out how satisfied you are with the services and treatment you received. Please respond to each statement by placing the number of the appropriate response in the blank space next to the statement.

1	2	3	4	5
Extremely dissatisfied	*Slightly dissatisfied*	*Neither satisfied nor dissatisfied*	*Slightly satisfied*	*Extremely satisfied*

How satisfied are you with:

_____ 1. The location of the office (store)

_____ 2. The parking around the office (store)

_____ 3. The scheduled office (store) hours

_____ 4. The office (store) atmosphere and decor

_____ 5. The telephone manners of the staff

_____ 6. The treatment you receive from the staff

_____ 7. The treatment you receive from the service provider

_____ 8. The prices for the services

_____ 9. The payment methods and terms

_____ 10. The quality of the services

_____ 11. The qualifications of the service provider

_____ 12. The manner in which your complaints are handled

_____ 13. The manner in which your questions are answered

_____ 14. The professionalism of the staff

_____ 15. The marketing and advertising programs of the service provider

NOTES

FOR OTHER FIFTY-MINUTE SELF-STUDY BOOKS
SEE THE BACK OF THIS BOOK.

NOTES

FOR OTHER FIFTY-MINUTE SELF-STUDY BOOKS
SEE THE BACK OF THIS BOOK.

We hope you enjoyed this book. If so, we have good news for you. This title is part of the best-selling *FIFTY-MINUTE*™ *Series* of books. All *Series* books are similar in size and identical in price. Several are supported with training videos (identified by the symbol **ⓥ** next to the title).

FIFTY-MINUTE Books and Videos are available from your distributor. A free catalog is available upon request from Crisp Publications, Inc., 1200 Hamilton Court, Menlo Park, California 94025.

FIFTY-MINUTE Series Books & Videos organized by general subject area.

Management Training:

ⓥ	Coaching & Counseling	68-8
	Conducting Training Sessions	193-7
	Delegating for Results	008-6
	Developing Instructional Design	076-0
ⓥ	Effective Meeting Skills	33-5
ⓥ	Empowerment	096-5
	Ethics in Business	69-6
	Goals & Goal Setting	183-X
	Handling the Difficult Employee	179-1
ⓥ	An Honest Day's Work: Motivating Employees	39-4
ⓥ	Increasing Employee Productivity	10-8
ⓥ	Leadership Skills for Women	62-9
	Learning to Lead	43-4
ⓥ	Managing Disagreement Constructively	41-6
ⓥ	Managing for Commitment	099-X
	Managing the Older Work Force	182-1
ⓥ	Managing Organizational Change	80-7
	Managing the Technical Employee	177-5
	Mentoring	123-6
ⓥ	The New Supervisor—Revised	120-1
	Personal Performance Contracts—Revised	12-2
ⓥ	Project Management	75-0
ⓥ	Quality at Work: A Personal Guide to Professional Standards	72-6
	Rate Your Skills As a Manager	101-5
	Recruiting Volunteers: A Guide for Nonprofits	141-4
	Risk Taking	076-9
	Selecting & Working with Consultants	87-4
	Self-Managing Teams	00-0
	Successful Negotiation—Revised	09-2
	Systematic Problem Solving & Decision Making	63-7

Management Training (continued):

Personal Improvement:

Human Resources & Wellness:

Human Resources & Wellness (continued):

Communications & Creativity:

Customer Service/Sales Training:

Small Business & Financial Planning:

Adult Literacy & Learning:

Career/Retirement & Life Planning: